TOPICS IN APPLIED GEOGRAPHY

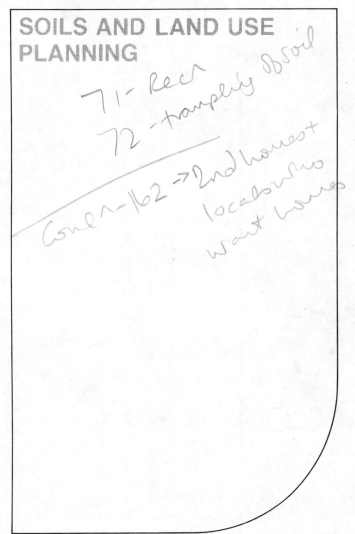

SOILS AND LAND USE PLANNING

TOPICS IN APPLIED GEOGRAPHY
edited by Donald Davidson and John Dawson

titles published and in preparation
Slum housing and residential renewal
Soil erosion
Human adjustment to the flood hazard
Office location and public policy
Vegetation productivity
Government and agriculture: a spatial perspective
Soils and land use planning
Pipelines and permafrost: physical geography and
    development in the circumpolar north

Donald A. Davidson
University of Strathclyde
Glasgow

SOILS AND LAND USE PLANNING

Longman
London
and New York

Longman Group Limited London

*Associated companies, branches and representatives
throughout the world*

*Published in the United States of America
by Longman Inc., New York*

© Donald A. Davidson 1980

First published 1980

British Library Cataloguing in Publication Data

Davidson, Donald A
  Soils and land use planning. –
  (Topics in applied geography).
  1. Land use – Planning   2. Soil science
  I. Title   II. Series
  333.7   HD111   79-40868

ISBN 0-582-48985-7

Printed in Great Britain by
Richard Clay (The Chaucer Press) Ltd, Bungay, Suffolk

CONTENTS

PREFACE

This book is based on an introductory course on applied pedology which I have taught at St David's University College, Lampeter, and at the University of Strathclyde, Glasgow. The aim of the course is to demonstrate to middle-level students how soil information can aid land use planning. The need for a short text on this topic is very apparent since none is available and relevant literature is scattered throughout a wide range of journals and reports. In the preparation for this book I became aware of the marked differences between various countries in the application of soil information to planning and thus I began to discern the need for a short text designed to encourage the broader use of soil survey data. It is thus very much the hope that the book will be useful not only to geography or other environmental science students interested in the application of pedology, but also to planners and members of planning committees who make decisions about the use of land.

I wish to thank all the authors who kindly sent me reprints of their work. In particular I am grateful to Mr R. Grant, Soil Survey of Scotland for providing the annotated aerial photograph for Fig. 2.1, and to Mr L. Lynch, Soil Conservation Service, New South Wales, for Figs 3.3 and 3.4. My study visit to the Netherlands in preparation for this book was made possible by financial assistance from the Carnegie Trust for the Universities of Scotland and from the University of Strathclyde. In the Netherlands I benefited from discussions with Professor A. P. A. Vink, Dr J. C. F. M. Haans and other members of the Soil Survey Institute. I am grateful to Mr C. J. M. Kraanen who arranged the details of my visit. I thank my co-editor, Dr J. A. Dawson, for his encouragement and comments on a draft of the text. Dr E. M. Bridges very kindly read the text for me and offered useful suggestions. Despite the help from all these friends, I alone am responsible for any errors or misrepresentations.

I am grateful to the secretarial services in the Department of Geography, University of Strathclyde, and in particular to Mrs M. MacLeod. The diagrams were drawn by the cartographers in this department and I wish to thank especially Mrs M. Walker for all her help. It is with pleasure that I also record the friendly collaboration with Mr I. Stevenson of Longman, not only with this book, but also with all the others in the series. In conclusion I acknowledge with affection all the support of my wife, Caroline, who has maintained domestic normality over recent months despite my sometimes erratic and remote behaviour and has also found time to correct and improve my English.

Donald A. Davidson
University of Strathclyde
April 1979

ACKNOWLEDGEMENTS

We are grateful to the following for permission to reproduce copyright material:

Agriculture Canada for our Fig 4.3 from a report by Coen and Holland 1976 published by Alberta Institute of Pedology and Agriculture; Table 2 from *Soils of Waterton Lakes* by Coen and Holland and Table 3 from *Guide for Assessing Soil Limitations for Playgrounds* by Coen and Holland; Department of Agriculture, Zambia for our Fig 4.1 from a report by Yager, Lee and Perfect 1967 Irrigation Map; Edward Arnold Publishers Ltd for an extract from *Evaluating the Human Environment* by Young; Canada Land Inventory for extracts from *Land Capability Analysis-Outaouais Area* 1972, Department of the Environment, and extracts from *Objectives, Scope and Organisation* Report No 1 Revised 1970, Department of Regional Economic Expansion; Commonwealth Scientific and Industrial Research Organisation for a soil map of Townsville plus legend by Murcha and Reid; Department of Agriculture and Fisheries for Scotland and Centre for Agricultural Strategy, University of Reading for data from *Land for Agriculture* to compile our Table 1.1; Department of Scientific and Industrial Research, New Zealand for an extract from *Framework of the New Zealand Method* by Leamy 1974, an extract from *Classification of Land Irrigation* by Griffiths 1975 and an extract from *Soils of Christchurch Region* by Raeside and Rennie 1974; Elsevier Scientific Publishing Co and the author, Dr. J. C. F. M. Haans for our Figs 5.6 and 5.8 from *Geoderma* 1970; Food and Agriculture Organization of the United Nations for extracts from *A Framework of Land Evaluation* and our Table 3.1 from *Land Evaluation in Europe*; The Institute of British Geographers for pp 109–111 from the article 'Land Judging Form' by Burnham and McRae in *Area* Vol 6 No 2; The Macaulay Institute for Soil Research for our Figs 2.1, 2.3b, 2.3c, Table 2.2 and a summarized extract published by the Soil Survey of Scotland, reproduced by permission of The Macaulay Institute for Soil Research and the authors; Macmillan Publishing Co Inc for our Fig 2.2 p 348 of *Nature and Properties of Soils* 8th Edition by Nyle C. Brady; Netherlands Soil Survey Institute for our Figs 5.1, 5.2, 5.3, 5.4a, b, c, d, e, f, 5.5, 5.7, Table 5.1, 5.2 and Appendix 3; Ordnance Survey for an aerial photograph and an extract from the Map and legend 1:63 360 Sheet 54, Crown Copyright Reserved; Oxford University Press for our Fig 2.4 from a paper by Dr. C. C. Rudiforth which appeared in *Journal of Soil Science* edited by Dr. A. Wild, published by Oxford University Press for the British Society of Soil Science; Soil Conservation Service New South Wales Government for our Figs 3.3 and 3.4 Computer Maps; Soil Conservation Society of America for our Table 4.1 by Bartelli from *Journal of Soil and Water Conservation* No 17 1962 copyright Soil Conservation Society of America; Springer

Verlag for an extract from *Land Use* by Vink, by permission of the Heidelberg Science Library; Transport and Road Research Laboratory for an extract from *Terrain Evaluation in West Malaysia* by Lawrance, reproduced by permission of the Director, Transport and Road Research Laboratory.

INTRODUCTION

The ever increasing pressure on land means that planning decisions ought to be made only after comprehensive analysis of all relevant factors. In terms of land use one such factor is the nature of the soil. This is most obvious in agriculture, but the assessment of soil conditions is also very relevant to the planning of other land uses, for example forestry and recreation. The long-standing emphasis of soil science has been on agriculture, but in recent years there has been a distinct broadening in application of the subject. The aim of this short book is to present an integrated review of soil assessment procedures based primarily upon the work which has been done in Western Europe, North America, Australia and New Zealand. The topic is very clearly one in applied geography since the focus is on methods of physical resource assessment relevant to land use planning. The hope is that this book demonstrates to geography and other environmental science students the application of soil expertise to the planning and management of land use. The intention is also to indicate to planners and to others who make land use decisions the types of useful information which soil scientists can provide.

As will be demonstrated in this book, the awareness of soil properties and how soils vary in space can be of tremendous advantage in the design of a land use plan. The incorporation of a soil input to planning has several merits. The ultimate costs of a plan can be better estimated if the physical difficulties are known; it is ecologically and aesthetically desirable for the design of an area to blend in with its natural environmental base, and when pressures are great on land, conservation demands that land most suitable to particular uses is retained for such purposes. In countries such as the Netherlands, Australia, Canada and the USA, there seems to be an awareness of the application of soil data to planning. In the Netherlands this is because of the extreme pressures on a limited land area as well as a strong national tradition in applied science. In Britain there is still much work to be done to publicise the importance and usefulness of soil to planning in the broadest sense.

The dominant theme in this book is how soil survey information can be interpreted and presented in a form helpful to land use planning. The book is designed for use on middle and upper university and polytechnic courses. The assumption is that the reader has completed a foundation course in physical geography or environmental science which included consideration of the basic nature and properties of soils. Readers without such backgrounds are referred to introductory texts such as those by Bridges (1977), Briggs (1977), Bunting (1972), Courtney and Trudgill (1976), Cruickshank (1972), FitzPatrick (1974), Jacks (1954) and Russell (1957). An introduction to British soils is given by Curtis, Courtney and Trudgill (1976). More advanced texts on soil science are provided by Brady (1974), FitzPatrick (1971), Foth and Turk (1972) and Russell (1973). Overall guidance on the literature of soil geography is given by Bridges (1977). Readers not familiar with soil survey work are urged to study any recent soil map and associated memoir produced by a national soil survey. Such a memoir not only describes the types of soil within the mapped area, but also the techniques used in the survey and usually some assessment of the various soils for land use purposes.

As will become apparent, there is a very wide literature dealing with the assessment of soils but there are few texts on the subject. Brook (1975) has compiled a bibliography of selected references for the period 1960 to 1972. The first major monograph was written by Jacks (1946), but this was not followed until the text by Bartelli *et al*. in 1966. It was only in the 1960s that techniques of land assessment began to be widely developed, tested and applied to different planning problems – reflected in the Bartelli *et al*. text and in a major symposium held in Canberra in 1966 which resulted in the volume by Stewart (1968). The first definitive text written by one author is by Vink (1975); another major contribution is by Young (1976), although this study is focused on the humid tropical environment. Whyte (1976) also draws together much of the material, but with an emphasis on South-East Asia. Another relevant text is by Mitchell (1973), though the emphasis in this book is on terrain analysis. An advanced text dealing very much with the principles and methodology of land evaluation is provided by Beek (1978).

A conference organised by the Agricultural Development and Advisory Service and the Soil Survey of England and Wales discussed the application of soil data to a variety of planning situations (Ministry of Agriculture, Fisheries and Food, 1974). A comprehensive review monograph on land classifications has been written by Olson (1974); review papers are provided by Trudgill and Briggs (1977) and Young (1978). A special issue of the journal *Photogrammetria* in 1970 was devoted to the topic of terrain classification and evaluation whilst the journal *Geoderma* focused attention on the non-agricultural applications of soil surveys (Simonson, 1974). The Welsh Soils Discussion Group devoted their conference papers in 1975–76 to the theme of soil survey interpretation and use and these papers have subsequently been published (Davidson, 1976a). A conference held at Cornell University has resulted in a useful publication entitled *Soil resource inventories* (1977). Albers, Krul and van Lanen (1975) compare various West European land classification systems.

This brief summary of the literature dealing with the subject in general terms is sufficient to illustrate the intensity of research effort and the virtual absence of introductory texts. The intention of this book is to fill this gap at least partially. Every attempt has been made to refer to all major publications concerned with soils and land use planning, but the vast number of research papers and reports necessitated a rather selective approach. Apologies are offered to scientists whose work is not referred to in this book. One danger in a book of this type is that full comprehension is only possible if the reader follows up a large number of the references. This is clearly undesirable from the undergraduate viewpoint and thus an outline is given wherever possible of most referenced publications. Nevertheless the reader would obviously benefit from following up references and also seeking out new publications by the use of such abstracting journals as *Soils and Fertilizers* and *Geoabstracts*.

In no way is this a book on planning, nor is its aim to make planners applied pedologists. Instead the hope is to show students of soils how their subject can be applied to land use planning and to indicate to planners the contribution which pedologists can make to their work. In this latter situation it is essential for planners to know the types of questions which a pedologist can tackle and thus it is important for planners to be aware of the spectrum of techniques at the disposal of the applied pedologist.

CHAPTER 1
SOIL RESOURCES AND PRESSURE ON LAND

'With increasing pressure on land, and a wakening political and popular awareness of environmental qualities, data on soil resources have become valuable tools in planning.' M. Ćirić (1975, p. 2)

1.1 INTRODUCTION

To a very large extent, research in soil science has been motivated by land use problems and this is particularly the case with the production of soil maps. Thus, soil science is clearly a practical or applied subject. This is not to deny that many soil scientists pursue research into topics which may appear to be extremely theoretical and remote from land use problems, but the underlying assumption is that such investigations can aid an understanding of pedogenic processes and may thus lead to practical benefits. In Britain serious interest in soil conditions first arose with the agricultural improvement movement in the eighteenth and early nineteenth centuries. During this period a series of county agricultural reports were produced by the first Board of Agriculture. For example, Keith (1811) was the first to produce a rudimentary soil map for Aberdeenshire; he also provided detailed descriptions of methods of land improvement and management which were in part conditioned by soil characteristics. In Britain during the nineteenth century the main advances in soil science were in agricultural chemistry and soil bacteriology – again orientated to the practical issue of soil fertility.

The foundations of *pedology* as a distinct subject area within soil science were established in the latter half of the nineteenth century by Vasilii Dokuchaev and his co-workers in Russia. In a strict sense pedology is the study of soils as they naturally occur in terms of their profile characteristics, spatial distribution and processes of formation. Dokuchaev and his team were commissioned to carry out various geological–geographical surveys and this led him to propose a classification of natural soils (Cruickshank, 1972). Thus such terms as podzol, sierozem, solonchak, and chernozem were introduced. In addition he proposed a conceptual framework whereby soils were interrelated with such characteristics as geology, geomorphology, hydrological conditions, climate, flora, fauna and man's activities.

The focus of this book is the application of soil information to land use planning. The various techniques which are used to evaluate the suitability of soil for specific land uses will be examined. It needs to be stressed that this will be approached from a *spatial* rather than a *site* context. This means that the resolution of the analysis will stop before the site level. In other words the concern is with assessing *areas* in terms of the soil problems posed to particular land uses. Investigation of soils and land use problems at the site level tend to be carried out by such specialists as a soil chemist, or a geotechnical engineer. Of course soil maps can only be produced by collecting information from sites, but then this information has to be spatially generalised, with the degree of generalisation depending upon such factors as the intensity of sampling, the complexity of the area and the scale of mapping. The role of soil survey or some form of base environmental inventory is thus critical in any land use planning programme. We shall examine the procedures used in a soil survey in Chapter 2, but it is instructive to outline the foundation of national surveys during the twentieth century.

Credit must be given to the Americans for executing the first modern scientific soil surveys. The US Soil Survey was founded in 1898 by Milton Whitney, but prominence is usually given to C. F. Marbut who became director in 1913. Marbut was a distinguished pedologist and made important contributions to soil classification. His basic division of soils into pedalfers and pedocals is still found to be useful (Young, 1976). In Canada the first proper soil surveys were carried out in 1921 beginning in Saskatchewan and Alberta; in Australia a start was made in 1927. In Britain it is surprising, given the agricultural changes of the eighteenth and nineteenth centuries and the rise of agricultural science, that a national soil survey was not formed until comparatively late. Some important pioneering work was done in the 1920s and 1930s, but the Soil Survey for England and Wales was not founded until 1939 (ultimately based at Rothamsted Experimental Station, Harpenden) and the Soil Survey for Scotland in 1946 (based at the Macaulay Institute, Aberdeen). It is only during the last thirty years that many soil maps have become available in Britain. In Scotland, for example, one-third of the country is covered by published 1 : 63 360 soil maps; maps and surveys in preparation bring the proportion up to about one-half of the country (Grant, pers. comm. 1978). It should be stressed that the emphasis in Scotland has always been on mapping the soils in dominantly arable areas and the published maps cover about 90 per cent of the arable land. In England and Wales soil maps are available at a scale of 1 : 63 360 for about one-tenth of the area, but a policy change in 1966 has led to the abandonment of the 1 : 63 360 scale in favour of the 1 : 25 000 scale; maps at this latter scale cover 2 per cent of the country. Another example is New Zealand with detailed soil maps at a scale of 1 : 15 840 or 1 : 31 680 covering approximately 5 per cent of the country whilst maps at the district level (scales 1 : 63 360 and 1 : 126 720) cover about 50 per cent (Leamy, 1974a). Soil maps at a scale of 1 : 253 440 cover the whole of New Zealand. At the global scale only about a fifth of the world's soils have been surveyed, but such a statistic masks tremendous variation (Dudal, 1978). If the arid regions and permafrost areas are excluded, 10.8 per cent of Africa has been mapped to compare, for example, with 80.2 per cent for Europe, 46.1 per cent for North and Central America, 15.0 per cent for South America and 28.2 per cent for the world (Dudal, 1978). These figures indicate that there is still a tremendous lack of basic soil survey data for many areas of the world.

In addition to the post-war trend of the rise in number of published soil surveys, other patterns can be discerned. The mapping of soils is only possible if use is made of a soil classification system. Many systems are now in use and are summarised in Bridges (1977), but mention must be made of the American system (Soil Survey Staff, 1975) which is becoming international in use as well as the legend which accompanies the *FAO–Unesco soil map of the world* (FAO, 1974a). The underlying dictates of newer classification systems are the desire to reduce subjective interpretation in assigning soils to specific types, to improve the basic store of data about individual soils and to ease comparison of soils from different areas. A consequence of new classification methods has been the introduction of many new terms which pose major problems to the users of soil maps. This difficulty has troubled many soil surveys since they are obviously keen that their maps should be used. One solution has been the production of interpretative maps – for example, in addition to a soil survey map being published, a map of land suitability or capability is also produced. This map shows the variation in grade of land with reference to one or more land uses. This topic will be given much greater consideration in later chapters.

The funding of most national soil surveys is by the relevant ministry of agriculture. Naturally, the work of soil surveys has been primarily orientated to agricultural purposes. However, the trend since the early 1960s has been the gradual recognition that soil survey data are applicable to many non-agricultural land uses, for example to forestry, recreation, wildlife, routes for roads, pipelines, and regional and urban planning. Some soil surveys have strongly' developed towards such increasing application of soil data. For example, the Netherlands Soil Survey includes a large department of applied soil survey. This broader approach is epitomised by the recent change in name of the Soil Research Institute in Ottawa, Canada, to the Land Resource Research Institute. One result of the increase in demand for soil data is the development of computer-based soil information systems, a topic to be discussed in Chapter 3. By such techniques soil data relevant to any land use problem can be quickly produced either in tabular or cartographic form.

This brief outline of the development of national soil surveys and the trends in new applications of survey data is sufficient to indicate the increasing importance which is being given to soils in aiding land use planning. Developments within pedology are encouraging the increasing use of soil information in planning, but the other side of the coin is that soil surveys are being increasingly approached by agencies or authorities to give advice on specific problems. Indeed a serious problem facing many soil research institutes is the extent to which soil surveyors' time can be devoted to such individual problems rather than carrying on with routine soil survey work. However, the requests for advice are not restricted to the local level – soil information is increasingly being sought at the local, regional, national and international scale. Although soil survey information is being used increasingly for non-agricultural land uses, without doubt the prime function of such surveys will always be towards agriculture. One force behind regional land use planning policies is the desire to maintain areas of particular agricultural value. Soil data are integral to the execution of such policies, a theme which we shall develop in the next section.

1.2 SOILS, AGRICULTURAL LAND AND PLANNING

Knowledge of soils is clearly integral to improving the management and output from existing agricultural areas as well as developing new localities. The planning of new arable areas, for example, requires information about the nutrient status of the soil so that appropriate types and quantities of fertilizers can be proposed. Also critical is the soil moisture regime in the rooting zone; many soils suffer from too much or too little moisture at critical periods during the farming year. Ultimate agricultural success will also depend on whether the soil is conducive to several crops being grown which can be fused into a profitable farming system. As already indicated, it is best to examine the incorporation of soil information into planning by considering various scales.

The global scale

Thomas Malthus in 1798 first drew attention to the tendency of people to increase in numbers at a geometric rate in contrast to the arithmetic rate of increase in food production. His pessimistic predictions were not realised because of technological, economic and sociological changes as well as by the opening up of new agricultural areas in North America and Australia, and the gradual introduction of birth control. His views have come to the fore again in recent decades resulting from a renewed concern with population trends and food supply, an issue which will intensify as we approach the twenty-first century. It is far beyond the scope of this book to enter into an analysis of this complex issue, but it is relevant to stress that any global land resource estimate can only be made if comprehensive soil information is available along with the specific soil requirements of different crops. Until very recently, soil maps covering the world based on soil surveys have been lacking and this explains in part why the estimates of the potential arable area of the world have been so variable. Grigg (1970) quotes studies dating from 1937 to 1958 which compare as percentages the global potential arable area with the arable area in use; the values range from 13 per cent to 375 per cent. In a more recent investigation of potentially arable soils of the world, Kellogg and Orvedal (1969) conclude that almost one-half of the soils in the world which have good physical and biological potential are already in use and they visualise soil surveys playing an important role in increasing productivity from such areas. In addition, according to their analysis, the areas of arable cultivation could be increased from c. 1.4 billion hectares to c. 3.2 billion hectares and this additional 1.8 billion hectares would not require additional irrigation beyond the existing wells and streams. Over one-half of this additional area lies in the tropics. This prediction by Kellogg and Orvedal is based on examination of major soil types and their distributions. Revelle (1976) in another analysis of global potentially arable land concludes that 3.2 billion hectares of land could be cropped without irrigation whilst this could be increased to 4.2 billion if irrigation systems were used. The most optimistic value for total arable area is 7.0 billion hectares (Pawley, 1971). As already stated, the marked variations in these estimates are in part due to a poor global soil and climatic data base as well as to differences in assumptions about management level, agricultural investment, economics of particular farming systems and the financial ability to buy fertilizers.

An important advance in terms of global land evaluation is under way by FAO (Dudal, 1978). The aim is to provide '. . . a more precise assessment of the production potential of the world's land resources, and so provide the physical data base necessary for planning future agricultural development . . .' (Dudal, 1978, p. 315). The work is based on the identification and delimitation of major agro-ecological zones. The background methodology to the evaluation procedure will be described in Chapter 3 where the FAO (1976) *Framework for Land Evaluation* is described. For the moment, it is important to realise that this global agro-ecological analysis is only possible through the publication in 1978 of the *FAO—Unesco Soil Map of the World*, published in nineteen sheets at a scale of 1 : 5 000 000. This project began in 1961 and necessitated much international collaboration and discussion of a legend and correlation of soils between countries. The maps were all published between 1974 and 1978 and are based on existing soil survey work throughout the world. These maps, in combination with a climatic assessment, will provide the basis for recognising agro-ecological types. Another example of the use of the 1 : 5 000 000 FAO–Unesco soil maps is given by Riquier (1975): he describes how the South America sheet has been digitised and additional information on climate, physiography, geology, vegetation, land use and land management is also stored for each soil unit. Such a data bank can then be used for a wide variety of land use problems.

This research by FAO should ultimately produce a comprehensive analysis of global land resources, and the preliminary results suggest that vast tracts of land are still available for cultivation (Dudal, 1978). However, it should always be borne in mind that the main hope for boosting world agricultural production must come from marked increases in yields from existing areas. Dudal also stresses that land evaluation exercises should be directed at the requirements of individual crops. An underlying difficulty to all global land resource appraisals is that countries vary in their socio-economic conditions and thus there will always be a marked difference between what could be achieved on scientific and technological evidence and what are realistic objectives within individual countries. Any predictions about food supply potential also can be outdated quickly by economic, technological or agricultural changes.

The national scale

Since there is no global government, land use planning backed by legislation at that scale is impossible. The world Food and Agriculture Organisation (FAO) acts as an important data-collecting centre and provides continuous reviews of the world food situation; FAO is also very much involved with agricultural development projects in various parts of the world. But it is at the national scale that a land use planning policy supported by legislation is first possible.

In Britain there is a long tradition of some form of control over land use. The first planning Act was passed in 1909, though its prime concern was with public health and housing. Further Acts followed in 1931 and 1932, but it was not until 1947 that comprehensive Acts were passed. These Town and Country Planning Acts (one for England and Wales and one for Scotland) imposed a statutory planning structure so that most forms of development had to receive planning permission from local authorities. Integral to these Acts was the zoning of land used for agriculture, and forestry. Various amendments were made to these Acts which were consolidated into the Town and Country Planning Act for England and Wales in 1971 followed by an Amendment Act in 1972. A separate Act for Scotland was passed in 1972. According to the 1947 Acts, authorities had to produce development plans which contained proposals on the use of land over a twenty-year period. Land was zoned for specific uses, for example green belts, and areas for urban, industrial, recreational and agricultural development and other community uses. The more recent 1971 and 1972 Acts provide a more positive approach to planning with the introduction of structure plans. These deal with strategic issues and policies for the development and the use of land. In addition detailed proposals for specific localities are presented in local plans. The procedure for such structure plans to become planning policy for specific areas is laid down fully within the Acts; before adoption, the plans must be available for public inspection and a method of objecting to any proposals is given in the Acts. In England and Wales the Ministry of Agriculture, Fisheries and Food, and in Scotland the Department of Agriculture and Fisheries, are consulted about such structure plans so that every attempt is made to conserve the best land for agriculture. As will be discussed, this policy seems to have worked reasonably well for England and Wales, but not in Scotland. Day-to-day planning is achieved by development control. This is when individual development proposals, for example extensions to private houses or the construction of new factories, are examined by the planning authorities. A variety of factors have to be taken into account including the policy statements in the strategic plan before planning permission can be granted. Planning authorities in England and Wales are obliged under the statute to consult the Ministry of Agriculture, Fisheries and Food when planning applications affect agriculture on areas greater than 5 ha. No such statutory requirement applies in Scotland, though the Secretary of State has issued a directive that planning authorities should consult the Department of Agriculture and Fisheries when areas greater than

5 ha and of grades A + and A are being considered for non-agricultural development. The report by the Centre for Agricultural Strategy (1976) identifies several unsatisfactory aspects of British planning procedures in relation to agriculture and forestry. According to their view 'there is insufficient consideration of the future consequences of land use changes in the context of national policies for agriculture, forestry and urban activities' (p. 18). They identify the problems of making the correct planning decisions at the local level in terms of national priorities. Another unsatisfactory feature of the planning process in Britain as noted in the report by the Centre for Agricultural Strategy (1976) is that the involvement in the planning process of those concerned with agriculture and forestry is inadequate. Indeed, the prime function of this report was to focus attention on the very high priority which should be given to food and timber production in Britain; in addition the report proposes '. . . that everything possible should be done both to prevent the unnecessary loss of land from agriculture and forestry and to stimulate the potential output per unit area from the land remaining in use for these purposes' (p. 16). Much of this concern results from the loss of land by urbanisation.

It has been estimated for the UK that if the population increases to 61 million by the year 2000, the demand for more urban land will mean between 163 000 and 468 000 ha being changed to this land use; the size range is because calculation has been done using different urban population densities and the areas are between 0.8 and 2.5 per cent of the agricultural area in 1974 (Centre for Agricultural Strategy, 1976). Although it seems as though this population projection may not be achieved and despite increasing attention being given to the redevelopment of inner city areas, a certain amount of urban expansion is bound to take place. The planning policy is to limit such development to poorer quality land wherever possible. For England and Wales this policy seems to have been moderately successful according to the work of Best (1973) who has shown that there has been no disproportionate loss of good-quality agricultural land though Best (1976) also argues that there should be a stronger policy designed to conserve better land for agriculture. The situation in Scotland seems rather different. As can be seen in Table 1.1, from 1971 until 1977 there has been a disproportionately high loss to agriculture of the better categories of land. Only 2.8 per cent of the total area of Scotland is in grade A + and A whilst from 1971/72 to 1976/77 between 17.5 and 29.0 per cent of the land transferred from agriculture was in these grades. Of course these figures must be interpreted with caution since in a strict sense they are not comparable, but it is clear that if such trends continue there will be a continuing loss of better agricultural land. Only for 1976/77 is there evidence of the poorest land (grade D) being more extensively used, but this figure for grade D results solely from one large industrial development.

In countries like Canada and the USA there is growing concern at the national level about the loss of good agricultural land to urbanisation. In the US until the early 1970s, there was the widespread belief that there was no need for concern about agricultural output. Continual increases in output were possible by the application of more fertilizers, new crop varieties and more efficient machinery. This view, expressed by Clawson (1972), has been challenged as a result of the marked increases in fuel and fertilizer costs in more recent years. In Canada, only about 15 per cent of the country has some potential for agriculture and less than 0.5per cent of this area can be considered to have prime soils in prime temperate climates (Nowland, 1978). This land is located in the Lakes Peninsula and the St Lawrence Lowlands. In Canada about 20 000 ha of land are being lost to urbanisation each year and the point that Nowland stresses is that most of this loss is taking place in the very limited areas of good land, a situation rather similar

Table 1.1 Land transfers in Scotland from agriculture to urban development by land quality (percentage of total) (Sources: For 1971/72 to 1974/75, Centre for Agricultural Strategy, 1976, p. 50: for 1975/76 and 1976/77, Department of Agriculture and Fisheries for Scotland, pers. comm., 1978).

YEAR	LAND GRADE						
	A+	A	B+	B	B−	C	D
1971/72	7.2	21.8	33.3	28.8	6.4	1.7	0.8
1972/73	4.9	14.9	37.3	32.9	8.2	1.1	0.7
1973/74	7.3	19.9	23.5	29.1	15.9	1.5	2.7
1974/75	6.2	18.8	25.4	25.2	12.2	4.7	7.5
1975/76	1.2	28.5	26.1	30.0	9.2	4.5	0.5
1976/77	7.0	10.5	22.0	13.0	7.5	3.0	37.0

Proportion of agricultural land in Scotland in each classification grade.

A+ 0.3%   B+ and B 13.5%   D 73.7%
A 2.5%   B− and C 10.0%

to Scotland. Land is graded by the Canada Land Inventory into seven classes with the first three classes being suitable for cultivation (Ch. 2). Nowland notes that over a half of Canada's class 1 agricultural land and one-third of the class 2 land is within 80 km of Canada's 23 metropolitan areas; the urban pressure on such land is thus obvious. The federal government has indicated its awareness of the need for some form of integrated national land use policy, but no legislation has yet emerged. As will be discussed later in this section, some legislative progress has been made at the provincial level in Canada.

In the USA there has been much discussion about the significance of the land which is lost to urbanisation. Hart (1976), in reviewing urban encroachment on rural areas, concludes that there is no serious immediate threat to the nation's supply of rural land and that the effect of urbanisation within the foreseeable future will not remove significant areas of land from agricultural production. But in no way does he relate the area lost to its agricultural significance, the point well demonstrated for Canada by Nowland (1978) and Bentley (1978). Indeed the United States Department of Agriculture has issued a policy statement which expresses concern at the loss of land well suited to the production of food, forage, fibre and timber (Knebel, 1976). In particular the USDA charges itself with advocating the protection of prime and unique farmlands, range, and forestlands from premature or unnecessary conversion to non-agricultural land use.

The state scale

Legislation for land use planning in countries with a federal structure, such as Canada and the USA, is dominantly at the state level. Land use planning control can be exerted in several ways; one method is to zone or reserve specific areas for agriculture, an approach adopted, for example, in parts of British Columbia and Newfoundland. Such designation requires that good agricultural land must be defined and delimited on maps, not always an easy task. Zoning of land for specific purposes is a very delicate issue and many states have failed to produce clear legislation on this matter. New York State introduced in 1971 an Agricultural District Programme which has received much popular as well as legislative approval (Lapping, 1975). The creation of such districts is initiated at the local level, and after individual districts are approved, the farmers in these areas benefit from a variety of tax and other benefits designed to encourage the long-term structure of farming. Without legislation such as this, agricultural land values round cities can become very high resulting in serious tax burdens for the farmers. This is because developers can offer sums of money for the land far in excess of its agricultural value. In fact, over forty states in the US have adopted legislation to ease in various ways the tax burden of such farmers, the hope being that such action will reduce the rate at which land is converted to urban uses (Collins, 1976). Another tactic used in American land use planning is the control of the spread of new housing areas by the denial of permits for the installation of septic tanks coupled with decisions not to extend sewers into selected areas (McCormack, 1974). The role of state governments in planning land use for agriculture can be considered in greater detail through an examination of the policies in Ontario, Alabama and California.

In 1977 the Government of Ontario produced a Green Paper on *Planning for agriculture: food land guidelines*. The underlying objectives of the paper are to preserve better land for agriculture and to ensure the economic feasibility of using the best land for agricultural production. Since this is a Green Paper, the aim is to produce a set of guidelines to assist planning authorities at subprovincial scales in making decisions over agricultural land. The key task is the identification of high capability agricultural resource lands which the Green Paper considers to include: (1) all lands which have a high capability for producing speciality crops (e.g. peaches, grapes, apples, tobacco, vegetables); (2) all lands where soil classes 1, 2, 3 and 4 predominate as defined in the Canada Land Inventory; (3) additional areas where farms exhibit characteristics of ongoing viable agriculture, and; (4) additional areas where local market conditions ensure agricultural viability where it might not otherwise exist. Following their identification these high capability agricultural areas have to be given a priority rating – for example speciality crop areas and lands of class 1 should be given top priority. After such a rating procedure, there must be an evaluation of alternative land uses. Areas designated for top agricultural priority must be mapped and given strong agricultural protection. On land in the second agricultural designation, some non-agricultural activities may be allowed. The Green Paper provides a discussion on agricultural policies, code of practice, compatible uses and severances for the highest priority agricultural designation. Clearly urban development, for example, is excluded from such areas.

The overall objective of the Ontario Green Paper is to give a policy directive for planning at the local, county or regional level so that the better agricultural areas are protected. The objectives of the Green Paper are highly commendable, but in practice a serious shortcoming of the Paper is that the land use decisions are made at the subprovincial level. Decisions at such a level may be made bearing local factors particularly in mind and without close reference to the agricultural needs of the state or indeed of the county as a whole. Another problem is that the Paper does not describe how land is to be assessed in a scientific and economic sense.

A similar concern to identify and protect what are termed 'critical areas' is implicit in recent legislation in the State of Alabama (Culver and Clonts, 1976). In 1973 an Environmental Land and Water Management Study Committee was established to study land resource management and land development regulation in the state. In 1975 an Act was introduced to protect defined critical areas such as prime agricultural land, floodplains, recreational areas, estuarine regions, wild and scenic rivers, wilderness areas and historical areas. Of particular interest in the present discussion is prime agricultural land defined as 'land that can be cultivated indefinitely with few hazards and limitations or requiring only moderate conservation practices' (Culver and Clonts, 1976, p. 11). This land coincides with class 1 land as defined by the USDA land capability scheme (Ch. 2). Only 3 per cent of the land area of Alabama falls in this category. Culver and Clonts (1976) visualise that some prime agricultural land will continue to be transferred to other uses even if land resource management policies are approved, but they stress that local land use decisions should be reviewed in aggregate at the state level. There are many similarities between the situation in Alabama and Ontario: both are feeling their way towards some form of state land use planning. General objectives of defining and conserving the best agricultural land are common to these states, but both have not produced the necessary Acts for such action.

In the USA the most explicit measure to preserve farmland is Assembly Bill 15 in California (Collins, 1976). At the time of Collins' paper (1976), the legislation had still to pass the California Senate and be signed by the governor. If the Bill had been passed, California would have been the first mainland state in the USA with state legislation to preserve agricultural land, with state supervision of agricultural land and with mandatory participation of agricultural landowners if their lands meet prime agricultural land status. This classification of land would have been carried out by a State Agricultural Resources Council – a body clearly missing in the Ontario and Alabama structures. Unfortunately the Bill failed in the California Senate by one vote, though the basic idea and principle are still alive (Collins, pers. comm. 1978).

The regional, county, township or local scale

As indicated for Canada and the USA, most planning decisions affecting land use are made by substate authorities. In fact in USA at substate level there are about 3 000 counties, 18 000 municipalities, 17 000 townships and some 488 substate districts which have some power to plan, influence or regulate land use (Collins, 1976). In Britain the planning structure seems more co-ordinated in part due to the small size of the country; for example in England there are 45 large county authorities within which there are 332 smaller district authorities, whilst in Scotland there are 9 regional authorities divided into 53 districts. Structure plans are prepared by the county authorities in England and Wales and by the regional authorities in Scotland whilst local plans which have to dovetail into the structure plan are usually prepared at the district level. We have already discussed how the quality of land for agriculture in Britain is taken into account in planning decisions, but a study by Gilg (1975) of planning decisions taken in a former Rural District Council in south-east Devon suggests that land grade did not appear to have much effect on development control.

In conclusion, it is interesting to consider the land use planning experience of one American county – Black Hawk County in north-central Iowa. The experience in this county, as described by Lex and Lex (1975) is instructive because not only is planning at this level illustrated, but also the conflicts of different parties, so common in land use planning, are very evident. The county is a prosperous agricultural area, based on the rich loessic soils, but pressure on this farmland has been exerted by the growing cities of Waterloo and Cedar Falls. The completion of a soil survey in 1973 coincided with the county being given permission to change its zoning ordinance. The soil survey information was then used as the basis for the calculation of a crop suitability rating which could be specified in the ordinance. The effect of the new proposed ordinance was to prohibit residential development on prime agricultural land as determined by the rating and to encourage such development on land of lower rating. Such a proposal was opposed at a public hearing by farmers and a realtor. Their fears were that growth would shift to adjacent counties at the expense of Black Hawk County. Farmers were concerned about the loss in their rights to determine the future of their land. The realtors' association, who finally were the only opposing group, wished to maintain their practice of selling land with as few restrictions as possible. In essence the realtors' group wished that prime agricultural land be defined so that it was of very limited extent whilst the planners wanted this land to be more extensive. Ultimately a decision was reached which meant that about 15 per cent of the farmland in Black Hawk County fell in this prime category; this land then became subject to the new rigorous land use planning ordinance. In their analysis of this county, Lex and Lex (1975) consider that this successful outcome was possible because of the availability of crop suitability ratings which were numerically based, thus allowing a compromise in the final definition of prime agricultural land, because of the role of planners in convincing farmers that there was the need for such an ordinance, and because of the influence of the chairman of the county commission, himself a farmer and an individual convinced of the need for agricultural land protection.

CHAPTER 2
SOIL SURVEY AND LAND USE CAPABILITY ASSESSMENT

2.1 SOIL SURVEY

The tasks of a soil survey are the description, classification, analysis and mapping of soils and, as described in Chapter 1, most countries have organisations charged with carrying out such studies. The focus of soil surveys traditionally has been towards agriculture, and thus soil usually is taken to be the natural medium within which plants will grow. However, the definition of soil as the plant rooting medium is rather limited. There is the question of the minimum depth of a soil – often unspecified, but, for example, the *System of soil classification for Canada* (Canada Soil Survey Committee, 1974) gives a minimum value of 10 cm. Plants obviously vary in their maximum rooting depths – another problem for defining soil precisely using the rooting zone concept. Soil information is being used increasingly for non-agricultural purposes, yet another reason for not using this definition. A more scientific definition can be suggested if soil is viewed as the result of soil-forming (pedogenic) processes which give it distinctive properties. A formal definition has been proposed by Joffe (1949) and has been slightly modified by Birkeland (1974, p. 3): 'a soil is described as a natural body consisting of layers or horizons of mineral and/or organic constituents of variable thicknesses, which differ from the parent material in their morphological, physical, chemical, and mineralogical properties and their biological characteristics.' In the investigation of soils, this means that the parent material ought always to be recognised and described; the uppermost part of this material and the overlying layers constitute the soil.

The starting point for most soil studies is the examination of a soil profile which is a vertical section from the surface to the parent material. The profile is composed usually of several horizons which are approximately parallel layers characterised by distinctive colour as well as by structure, texture, consistence, and chemical, biological and mineralogical composition. Even within a soil pit of 1 m in width, marked variations in depth of horizons can occur and this stresses the three-dimensional nature of soil. The two-dimensional unit of study is a soil profile, whilst the smallest three-dimensional unit is called a *pedon*. A pedon is the smallest volume which can be considered a soil and the surface extent varies from about 1 to 10 m² (Brady, 1974). For mapping soils it is clearly impossible to indicate variation in individual pedons; instead similar pedons have to be grouped into *polypedons* and these form the basis of soil mapping. The aim of a soil survey must be to recognise mapping units or polypedons made up of pedons which are comparatively similar in terms of horizon types and sequences, and parent material. Soil maps at the scale of 1 : 50 000 or 1 : 63 360 usually show the distribution of soil series which are named after a local type-site. A soil series is a group of soils with similar profiles developed on similar parent materials. We shall return later in this subsection to soil classification, but it is important to stress that soils are three-dimensionally variable phenomena. The characterisation of a soil series by the description of a representative profile is an attempt to describe the dominant pedon present, but quantitative information is not usually given in a soil survey report about deviation from this norm. Webster (1977) suggests that it is not reasonable to expect more than 60 per cent of the soil in any one mapping unit to belong to the type of profile which the unit is supposed to exhibit.

The variability and complexity of soils in any area presents the surveyor with a major sampling problem. Descriptions of sampling methods are given by Bridges (1978), Clarke (1971), Hodgson (1978) and Smith and Atkinson (1975). The most comprehensive discussion of sampling and indeed of all aspects of soil survey procedure is given by the Soil Survey Staff (1960) of the US Department of Agriculture. For present purposes, a brief outline of field procedures is appropriate. The reader is also encouraged to study any soil memoir since such a book always summarises the methods used in that particular soil survey.

Prior to any soil survey, the surveyor will familiarise himself with the climate, geology, geomorphology, vegetation, land use and land use history of the area. No doubt he will deepen his feel for the area by the examination of aerial photographs and any other remote sensing imagery as well as by making reconnaissance traverses. Most soil maps have been produced by the interpretative approach to sampling. In essence this involves the surveyor in identifying landscape units which would appear to him to be homogeneous in terms of soils. This is done by the recognition of morphological, geomorphological and vegetational units in the landscape. For example, he might recognise a recurring set of slope units in a valley and this would lead him to delimit these units and to sample them in turn for their soils. The close association between soils and morphology is of prime assistance, not only in subdividing the landscape into areas for soil sampling but also for ultimately guiding the mapping of the soils. However, the surveyor also must be closely influenced in his subdivision of the landscape by variations in the other environmental characteristics. In this regard aerial photographs are particularly useful since differences in tones and textures directly indicate variations in vegetation, drainage conditions and soils. As the surveyor becomes increasingly familiar with his area, he will make greater and greater use of aerial photographs for guiding his field sampling and for drawing in the boundaries between soil series. Figure 2.1 demonstrates the use of an aerial photo for soil mapping. A comprehensive description of the use of aerial photographs in soil surveys is provided by Carroll, Evans and Bendelow (1977).

This interpretative approach to selection of sites at which soils are investigated is essentially a stratified sampling design. Other sampling techniques are line traverses and systematic designs. As an example of the latter, Rudeforth and Bradley (1972) have

Fig. 2.1 An example of an aerial photograph used in a soil survey. The location of the area indicated by the square in the centre is shown in Fig. 2.3a. The surveyor draws boundaries round areas which appear to be uniform landscape units on the basis of photo patterns and tones. A field sampling programme is then planned in order to collect information about the photo units and to check on the boundaries. The surveyor records the location of investigated sites on the photographs (not included in the extract) and is able to finalise the boundaries between his mapping units (soil series). A key to the soil series in the extract is given in the caption to Fig. 2.3b (page 27). (Soil survey information kindly supplied by Mr R. Grant, Soil Survey of Scotland.) Crown Copyright Reserved.

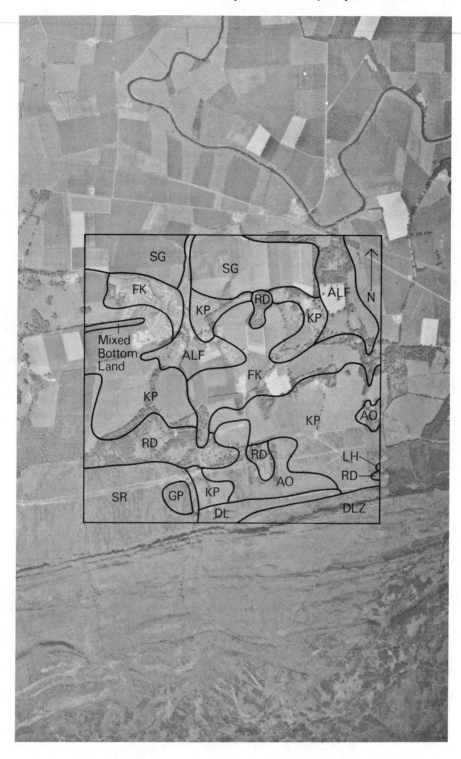

sampled on a 1 km grid interval the soils of west and central Pembrokeshire in West Wales. At each of their *c.* 1 000 grid intersections, they examined the soil.

Irrespective of sampling design, it is essential that there are standard procedures for describing soils to ensure that observations by different surveyors are comparable. This means that every national Soil Survey has to instruct its surveyors to use a particular field manual. Soil profile information, besides being described in a standard manner, has also to be recorded in a similar way to permit manual or computer storage and retrieval of profile descriptions. For example, the Soil Survey for England and Wales uses the *Soil Survey Field Handbook* compiled and edited by Hodgson (1974). In summary, the full description of a site and soil using this method would produce data under the headings listed below. Terms marked with an asterisk are described in the glossary (Appendix 1); full definitions of all terms are given in the *Soil Survey Field Handbook* (Hodgson, 1974).

1. *General and site description*
   Grid reference
   Elevation
   Slope (value, aspect and form)
   Soil erosion and deposition
   Rock outcrops (extent of exposed bedrock)
   Land use
   Soil surface (form, condition, thickness of litter (L) horizon)
   Bedrock (lithology, structure, hardness, colour)

2. *Profile description (for each horizon)*
   Lower depth
   Colour* (moist soil, ped* face, air-dry, rubbed and main mottles)
   Mottles* (abundance, size, contrast, sharpness)
   Organic matter status
   Particle-size* class
   Stones (size, abundance, shape, lithology)
   Soil-water state
   Ped* (size, shape, grade)
   Voids* (packing density, porosity class, fissures, macropores)
   Consistence* (soil strength, ped strength, failure, cementation, stickiness, plasticity)
   Roots (size, abundance, nature)
   Nature of 0 (peaty) horizon
   Nodules* (composition and nature, abundance, shape)
   Coats* (kind, abundance)
   Horizon boundary* (distinctiveness, form)
   Horizon notation*
   Sample number

This field data combined with results from laboratory analysis allows the soil surveyor, after some experience, to assign each site to a soil series. On the basis of aerial photo interpretation and field observation he would draw the boundaries between the soil mapping units as on Fig. 2.1. As already stressed, such mapping units will contain more than one series, but one should be dominant, otherwise the unit is mapped as a complex. Soil mapping is only possible if a soil classification system is used. There are methods of numerical taxonomy whereby statistical procedures are followed in order to identify which profiles are most similar to each other, but such techniques are not used in routine soil survey work. Instead, soil surveys use some defined hierarchical system. For example the soil classification system for England and Wales (Avery, 1973) has the following levels:

Major group (e.g. lithomorphic soils, brown soils, podzolic soils, pelosols, etc.)
Group   (e.g. rankers, rendzinas, brown calcareous earths, brown podzolic soils, stagnopodzols, etc.)
Sub-group   (e.g. humic ranker, brown rendzina, gleyic brown calcareous earth, paleo-argillic brown podzolic soil, ironpan stagnopodzol, etc.)
Soil series (named after type sites, e.g. Hanslope series, Stretham series, etc.)

Reference should also be made to the FAO–Unesco scheme (FAO, 1974a), the American method (Soil Survey Staff, 1975), the Canadian method (Canadian Department of Agriculture, 1974; Canada Soil Survey Committee, 1978), and the Australian system (Stace *et al.*, 1968; Northcote, 1974). Quite clearly even a brief description of these schemes is beyond the scope of this book; an introduction to soil classification is given by Bridges (1978) and McRae and Burnham (1976).

It has been assumed so far that soil maps result primarily from detailed soil survey work. Soil maps, of course, vary in scale, and level of generalisation. Maps in the scale range from 1 : 10 000 to 1 : 2 500 or more require *intensive* surveys following FAO practice as described by Webster (1977); the scale range 1 : 25 000 to 1 : 10 000 requires *detailed* field survey whilst the next range up to 1 : 100 000 needs a semi-detailed survey. Scales smaller than 1 : 100 000 are based on a *reconnaissance* survey. Maps of 1 : 25 000 and larger use phases of soil series as well as soil series as the mapping units. Phases cannot normally be shown in the scale range 1 : 25 000 to 1 : 100 000 when soil series and associations of soil series provide the mapping units. At scales smaller than 1 : 100 000, groups, major groups or some type of physiographic assemblage are the mapping units. As published map scales become smaller, so the minimum size of a particular mapping unit which can be shown increases (Table 2.1).

One important aspect of soil survey which has not been considered is the intensity of sampling. This is obviously related to the scale of the map to be published, the objective of the survey, the complexity of the area and the financial and labour resources

Table 2.1   Minimum-size delineation values on actual ground scale for a number of map scales (minimum-size delineations for all published maps being 0.4 cm²) (From Eswaran, Forbes and Laker, 1977, p. 41).

MAP SCALE	MINIMUM-SIZE DELINEATIONS ON GROUND SCALE (ha)
1 : 5 000 000	100 750
1 : 1 000 000	4 030
1 : 500 000	1 008
1 : 250 000	252
1 : 200 000	161
1 : 100 000	40.3
1 : 50 000	10.1
1 : 25 000	2.52
1 : 20 000	1.61
1 : 10 000	0.40

of the survey organisation. A very rough guide to sampling intensity is given by Webster (1977) who suggests 5.00 observations per cm^2 of map though he appreciates that judicious use of other information combined with the nature of the area may make less than 5.00 observations per cm^2 perfectly adequate. Surveyors in the Soil Survey of England and Wales use field maps at a scale of 1 : 10 560 and the ultimate published maps are at 1 : 25 000. In Britain experienced surveyors make about 30–60 soil observations per km^2 (Beckett, 1978) which is equivalent to 1.88 to 3.75 observations per cm^2 of published map. Only with junior staff of less experience does the intensity rise up to 5.00 observations per cm^2. In considering the precision of soil mapping, it is important to consider not only the scale of the map but also the density of observations – indeed some researchers (Steur, 1961; Vink, 1963a) believe that the latter is a better indication of detail than scale. But having a high intensity of observation is a very inefficient method of increasing map precision since sampling intensity should vary according to the variability of the soils in a study area. Indeed Nortcliff (1978) has demonstrated that soil survey procedures do not take sufficient account of soil variability and that reconnaissance surveys should be carried out to determine sampling intensities.

It can be readily appreciated that a soil map, along with its associated memoir, contains a great deal of highly compressed, scientific information about the soils of an area. The development of classification methods which introduce many new terms, as well as the increasing use of detailed schemes of soil profile description, means that workers other than soil scientists encounter many problems in trying to understand and extract relevant information from a soil map and memoir. As explained in Chapter 1, there is an increasing demand for soil information, yet developments in soil survey are in a sense making such information not readily accessible in a suitable form. This problem is recognised widely by soil surveys and one response has been the publication of land capability maps.

2.2 LAND CAPABILITY – THE AMERICAN METHOD

The American method of land capability assessment has evolved over c. 30 years. An early review of the research was given by Hockensmith and Steele (1949), but it was not until 1961 that a comprehensive handbook was published (Klingebiel and Montgomery, 1961). The technique was evolved by the Soil Conservation Service of the US Department of Agriculture. For brevity the system will be referred to as the USDA method. Summaries of this method are given by Hudson (1971), Young (1973, 1976), Olson (1974) and Brady (1974). Integral to the assessment procedure is an evaluation of soil erosion hazards, wetness and soil and climatic limitations. The need for such an assessment became very evident in the US with the soil erosional problems especially in the Mid-west in the 1930s.

It should be stressed at this stage that land capability assessment is based on a broader range of characteristics than just pure soil properties. General methodological issues about land evaluation will be discussed in Chapter 3. Land capability assessment utilises information on slope angle, climate, flood and erosion risk, as well as on soil properties. Of course, there is a large degree of interrelation between these types of information and thus to a very large extent soil mapping units are grouped together to form capability units.

The prime aim of the method is to assess the degree of limitation to land use or potential imposed by land characteristics on the basis of permanent properties. A scale

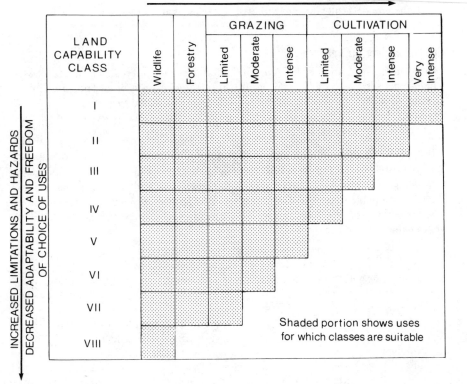

Fig. 2.2 Intensity with which each land capability class can be used with safety. Note the increasing limitations on the uses to which the land can safely be put as one moves from class I to class VIII (From Nyle C. Brady: *The Nature and Properties of Soils*, 8th Edition, p. 348, Macmillan Publishing Co. Inc.).

of land capability grades can thus be envisaged with the degree of limitation and hazard defining the classes. This concept is illustrated in Fig. 2.2 with the eight classes of the USDA method. As the degree of limitation increases, so the range of land use options decreases. Comment needs to be made about the nature of permanent properties. The capability assessment would become quickly redundant if the values of selected properties could easily be changed. For example, a farmer can quickly change the pH value of his fields by the application of lime. In contrast, it is far more difficult for him to modify the slope of his land, the depth of his soil, the effects of past erosion, soil texture, type of clay minerals and water-holding capacity. If it is technically and economically feasible to tackle such problems as water lying on the surface of the soil, lack or excess of water in the soil, stones, presence of soluble salts or exchangeable sodium or a hazard of overflow, then these limitations are considered not permanent. Under such circumstances these limitations would not be taken into account in capability assessment. Clearly there are difficulties in deciding what is technically and economically feasible and an additional problem is that technical and economic changes mean that any land capability assessment will have to be reappraised.

The USDA method has three levels in its classification structure.

(i) Capability class

This is the broadest category and a total of eight classes are defined and labelled I to VIII inclusive.

(ii) Capability subclass

These subclasses indicate the type of limitations encountered within the classes. Limitations such as an erosional hazard, rooting zone restriction, and problems of climate, stoniness, low fertility, salinity or wetness are indicated by a letter subscript. For example, class V with major limitations imposed by excess water and climatic characteristics is indicated as Vwc.

(iii) Capability unit

This is a subdivision of the subclass. Land in one capability unit clearly includes many different soils but has little variation in *degree* and *type* of limitation to land use, but in addition is suitable for similar crops under similar farm and soil management schemes. The yield range of crops within capability units in such circumstances should not be greater than 25 per cent.

The assignment of any soil mapping unit to a capability class, subclass or unit is only possible if a number of assumptions are made and these are specified fully by Klingebiel and Montgomery (1961). It is important to reiterate the underlying assumption that soils of different type may well be grouped into the same capability class since they share the same *degree* of limitation. Comments about suitability for specific crops can only be made at the level of the capability unit. A moderately high level of management is assumed on the part of the land users. This level is considered to be 'reasonable' for the area in question. Greater variations in management techniques may well be required within capability classes than between classes. This is because of the variations in soil mapping units which can be grouped together in terms of capability class. Factors such as distance to market, types of roads, size and shape of the soil areas, location within fields, ability and resources of individual land users, and other characteristics of land ownership are not taken into account.

Klingebiel and Montgomery (1961) provide a full description of the type of land within each of the eight capability classes. The brief summary of these classes as provided by Young (1973, pp. 14–15) is given below. The close association between the abbreviated definitions and Fig. 2.2 should be evident. Note that classes I to IV are cultivable whilst the remaining classes are not.

Class I   Soils with few limitations that restrict their use.
Class II   Soils with some limitations that reduce the choice of plants or require moderate conservation practices.
Class III   Soils with severe limitations that reduce the choice of plants or require special conservation practices, or both.
Class IV   Soils with very severe limitations that restrict the choice of plants, require very careful management, or both.
Class V   Soils with little or no erosion hazard, but with other limitations impractical to remove, that limit their use largely to pasture, range, woodland or wildlife food and cover. (In practice this class is mainly used for level valley-floor lands that are swampy or subject to frequent flooding.)
Class VI   Soils with very severe limitations that make them generally unsuited to cultivation and limit their use largely to pasture or range, woodland or wildlife.

Class VII   Soils with very severe limitations that make then unsuited to cultivation and restrict their use largely to grazing, woodland or wildlife.

Class VIII   Soils and landforms with limitations that preclude their use for commercial plant production and restrict it to recreation, wildlife, water supply or aesthetic purposes

If the USDA method is considered as a fully defined land classification technique, then it can be severely criticised. If the descriptions of the capability classes are examined, a distinct lack of precise quantitative criteria will quickly be very evident. Phrases such as 'gentle slopes', 'moderate susceptibility to wind or water erosion or 'less than ideal soil depth' clearly lack precision of definition, thus making them liable to diversity of interpretation. However, it can be argued that the strength of the USDA method lies in its flexibility, a viewpoint put forward by Young (1973). Major difficulties arise if any attempt is made to fix rigid limiting values which are relevant to a variety of environments. Consider soil texture: the significance of the textural types (loam, sandy loam, clay loam, etc.) will vary according to the climatic regime and to the types of crops or land uses. Thus the lack of precise limiting values gives the USDA method distinct flexibility. The method is better described as a *framework* for land capability assessment since it can be adapted for a wide variety of environmental conditions. Young and Goldsmith (1977) do such an exercise for part of Malaŵi.

The hopes of Hockensmith and Steele (1949) about the potential uses of land capability maps have been realised to a large extent. They visualised such maps being used by farmers for a wide variety of purposes, by soil conservation officers to determine the conservation needs, both at the regional and individual farm levels, and by taxation authorities or lending institutions requiring information about the basic nature of land. Practically all soil survey reports in the US contain a section on land capability and this information is used widely by advisory and planning agencies. As described in Chapter 1, a concern in many states of the US is the definition and delimitation of Prime Agricultural Land which will subsequently come under some particular legislation designed to protect it. Data on land capability are often used for this purpose, though additional considerations such as proximity to markets, availability of transport facilities and land use practices in adjoining areas are also taken into account.

2.3 LAND CAPABILITY – THE CANADIAN METHOD

Land capability assessment in Canada was initiated by the Canada Land Inventory which was established in 1963 as a result of the Agricultural Rehabilitation and Development Act (ARDA) of 1961. This Inventory is a comprehensive survey of land capability and use designed to provide a basis for resource and land use planning (Canada Land Inventory, 1970). It is meant to be used for planning rather than for management at the municipal, provincial and federal levels. The Inventory is very much a generalised or reconnaissance assessment and cannot provide sufficiently detailed information at the local level. The survey covers all the settled and adjacent areas of Canada, amounting to about 2 500 000 km².

The general approach of the Canadian land capability scheme is modelled on the USDA method, though some important differences must be stressed. Besides there being a method of soil capability classification for agriculture, there are separate land capability assessment schemes for forestry, recreation and wildlife – further separated into ungulates and waterfowl. The species of ungulates (antelope, caribou, deer, moutain goat, moose and mountain sheep) indicate how the capability scheme has been tailored to Canadian conditions. For illustrative purposes a brief outline is given below of the agriculture and recreation capability schemes; a complete summary of the schemes is provided by Report No. 1 of the Canada Land Inventory (1970). Reports on the individual schemes are also available.

All the Canadian capability schemes have seven classes in contrast to the eight of the USDA method. The soil capability classes for agriculture can be summarised as follows:

Classes

1 Soils in this class have no significant limitations in use for crops

The soils are deep, are well to imperfectly drained, hold moisture well and in the virgin state were well supplied with plant nutrients. They can be managed and cropped without difficulty. Under good management they are moderately high to high in productivity for a wide range of field crops.

2 Soils in this class have moderate limitations that restrict the range of crops or require moderate conservation practices

The soils are deep and hold moisture well. The limitations are moderate and the soils can be managed and cropped with little difficulty. Under good management they are moderately high to high in productivity for a fairly wide range of crops.

3 Soils in this class have moderately severe limitations that restrict the range of crops or require special conservation practices

The limitations are more severe than for class 2 soils. They affect one or more of the following practices: timing and ease of tillage; planting and harvesting; choice of crops; and methods of conservation. Under good management they are fair to moderately high in productivity for a fair range of crops.

4 Soils in this class have severe limitations that restrict the range of crops or require special conservation practices, or both

The limitations seriously affect one or more of the following practices: timing and ease of tillage; planting and harvesting; choice of crops; and methods of conservation. The soils are low to fair in productivity for a fair range of crops, but may have high productivity for a specially adapted crop.

5 Soils in this class have very severe limitations that restrict their capability to producing perennial forage crops, and improvement practices are feasible

The limitations are so severe that the soils are not capable of use for sustained production of annual field crops. The soils are capable of producing native or tame species of perennial forage plants, and may be improved by use of farm machinery. The improvement practices may include clearing of bush, cultivation, seeding, fertilizing or water control.

6 Soils in this class are capable only of producing perennial forage crops and improvement practices are not feasible

The soils provide some sustained grazing for farm animals, but the limitations are so severe that improvement by use of farm machinery is impractical. The terrain may be unsuitable for use of farm machinery, or the soils may not respond to improvement, or the grazing season may be very short.

7 Soils in this class have no capability for arable culture or permanent pasture

This class also includes rockland, other non-soil areas and bodies of water too small to show on the maps.

0 Organic soils (not placed in capability classes)

(Canada Land Inventory, 1970, pp. 23–4)

As with the USDA method subclasses are indicated by letters. The Canadian method has a wider range of such limitations than the USDA one. The background assumptions to the Canadian scheme are very similar to those of the USDA method.

In the scheme for classifying land according to recreation capability, the seven classes are differentiated according to the intensity of outdoor recreational use, or the quantity of outdoor recreation which may be generated and sustained per unit of land per annum under perfect market conditions. This last point means that a uniform demand and accessibility is assumed for all areas – in other words location relative to population centres and to existing access are not included in the assessment procedure. The capability classes for recreation can be summarised as follows:

Classes

1 Lands in this class have very high capability for outdoor recreation

Class 1 lands have natural capability to engender and sustain very high annual use based on one or more recreational activities of an intensive nature.

Class 1 land units should be able to generate and sustain a level of use comparable to that evident at an outstanding and large bathing beach or a nationally known ski slope.

2 Lands in this class have a high capability for outdoor recreation

Class 2 lands have natural capability to engender and sustain high annual use based on one or more recreational activities of an intensive nature.

3 Lands in this class have a moderately high capability for outdoor recreation

Class 3 lands have natural capability to engender and sustain moderately high annual use based usually on intensive or moderately intensive activities.

4 Lands in this class have moderate capability for outdoor recreation

Class 4 lands have natural capability to engender and sustain moderate annual use based usually on dispersed activities.

5 Lands in this class have moderately low capability for outdoor recreation

Class 5 lands have natural capability to engender and sustain a moderately low total annual use based on dispersed activities.

6 Lands in this class have low capability for outdoor recreation

Class 6 lands lack the natural quality and significant features to rate higher, but have the natural capability to engender and sustain low annual use based on dispersed activities.

7 Lands in this class have very low capability for outdoor recreation

Class 7 lands have practically no capability for any popular types of recreation activity, but there may be some capability for very specialised activities with recreation aspects, or they may simply provide open space.

(Canada Land Inventory, 1970, pp. 33–4)

Again, subclasses are defined using a letter notation. Some examples are E (land with vegetation possessing recreational value), F (waterfall or rapids), G (significant glacier view or similar experience) and H (historic or prehistoric site). It can be readily appreciated that the interpretation of *land* varies according to the capability method. With the land capability classification for ungulates, for example, land is categorised according to its habitat suitability for these particular animals.

Besides the publication of maps showing land classified according to these different schemes, an attempt is also made to synthesise the information into one overall assessment. The aim is to present one integrated map which proposes the best land use based on capability. Such a map is directed at regional land use planning and development. The detailed methodology of such an analysis will vary from area to area, but it is instructive to outline the procedure which was adopted for the land capability analysis of the Outaouais region – a large part of Quebec to the west of Montreal. This map by the Canada Land Inventory is published at a scale of 1 : 250 000. The methodology used in the land capability analysis is taken from the supporting description to the map.

The analysis of land use capability was carried out in three stages.

1. The first was the blocking of sectoral maps aimed at isolating the best zones in each sector, and regrouping the identified classes in categories represented by the letters *a*, *b* and *c*, except in the wildlife sector. The classes were regrouped as follows:

SECTOR	CATEGORY *a*	CATEGORY *b*	CATEGORY *c*	CLASSES NOT RETAINED
Agriculture	Classes 1, 2, 3	Class 4	Class 5	Classes 6, 7
Forestry	Classes 1, 2, 3	Class 4	Class 5	Classes 6, 7
Recreation	Classes 1, 2	Class 3	Class 4	Classes 5, 6, 7
Wildlife, ungulates			Classes 2W and 3W*	
Wildlife, waterfowl			Classes 1, 2, 3, 4, 3M†	

*2W and 3W   Lands in this special class are class 2 and class 3 areas respectively, that are winter ranges on which animals from surrounding areas depend.

†3M   Class 3 land for wildlife/waterfowl which suffers from poor water-holding capacity of soils thus adversely affecting the formation and permanency of water areas.

2. A second stage was necessary in the preparation of the synthesis map for agriculture. This stage consisted of a comparison between the capability maps and the land use map in order to evaluate the amount of cleared land. After this comparison, the category *a* soils (classes 1, 2, 3) used by agriculture were mapped. The zones of category *b* and *c* (classes 4, 5) were studied in the field with local agronomists. Lands of these categories that are presently extensively cultivated were mapped as

agricultural zones: lands represented on the land use maps as abandoned were identified as agricultural and denoted by the letter 'x'. This symbol signifies that the information collected to date is insufficient, and that more precise studies of a socio-economic and geophysical nature should be effected before agricultural use is confirmed or an alternate use suggested. The zones in which agriculture is rapidly disappearing were treated in the same manner as uncleared land with agricultural potential and were not shown on the map as agricultural.

3. The third step was the actual zoning on the integrated map. First, the urban zones were traced on the base map after consulting the present land use map. Secondly, the recreational zones were added as they appeared on the blocked map for this sector. Recreational zones were given priority because of their high intensity of use per unit area. Next, the agricultural zones, as previously established, were traced on the integrated map. The forestry capability was then transcribed in the remaining blank spaces. Wintering areas used by ungulates were indicated in the forest zones. In the marshy areas, usually unclaimed by other land uses, were the zones of importance to waterfowl. Finally, the spaces not claimed by any other sector were designated as zones of low potential.

It can be readily appreciated that such an overall analysis in combination with the land capability maps very much aids regional land use planning. At the national scale problems arise in comparing classes of land between very contrasting areas. For example, class 1 land for agriculture in the prairies will not support the same range of crops nor give as good yields as the same class of land in Ontario because of rainfall and growing season differences (Nowland, 1978). In other words, the climatic considerations in the capability scheme are not sufficiently rigorous and Nowland (1978) in his analysis of Canada's agricultural land resources uses an agroclimatic assessment in addition to the soil capability assessment. Other developments in Canada for assessing land in connection with land use planning will be discussed in Chapters 3 and 4.

2.4 LAND CAPABILITY – THE BRITISH METHOD

Before attention is focused on the method developed and used by the Soil Survey in Britain, mention must be made of other approaches. The first national assessment of land grade resulted from the Land Utilisation Survey in the 1940s (Stamp, 1962). Under this method land was graded on the basis primarily of land use characteristics and maps at a scale of 1 : 625 000 were published. Such information, albeit very generalised and subjective, was all that was available to assist land use planning in the 1950s. By the 1960s there was the growing realisation that a more detailed and up-to-date assessment of land was needed. A study group was established in 1962 under the aegis of the Agricultural Land Service of the Ministry of Agriculture, Fisheries and Food, and an *Agricultural Land Classification* was published in 1966. In this scheme land is graded into five classes according to degree of limitation imposed by soil and climatic conditions on agriculture. The degree of limitation is expressed in terms of range of crops which can be grown, the level of yield, the consistency of yield and cost of obtaining the yield (Morgan, 1974). Agricultural land classification maps at a scale of 1 : 63 360 are available for England and Wales. The prime objective of these maps is to assist planning decisions concerning the release of agricultural land for urban purposes. One problem with this scheme is that almost one-half of the agricultural land in England and Wales has been classed as grade 3. More detailed assessment of this grade has proved necessary and a scheme is now available for defining and identifying three subgrades of grade 3 (Agricultural Development and Advisory Service, 1976). A summary and review of the agricultural land classification scheme are provided by Morgan (1974). In Scotland the Department of Agriculture and Fisheries has not published agricultural land classification maps, though information using a A+, A, B+, B, B−, C and D scale (Table 1.1) is made available to planning authorities. These lettered grades correspond to very good, good, medium plus, medium, medium minus, poor and non-arable land respectively. The grading is based on a field visual survey supported by information on productivity of various farms.

In Britain the Soil Survey has developed a Land Use Capability Classification (Bibby and Mackney, 1969), modelled on the USDA scheme. The factors which led to such a development in the Soil Survey are very similar to those described for the USA and Canada. In particular the prime aim was to present the results of soil surveys in a form suitable for planners, agricultural advisers, farmers and other land users. As with the American and Canadian schemes, a number of assumptions are specified in the British scheme. For example, the classification is primarily for agricultural purposes. A moderately high level of management is assumed. Land is only graded on the basis of limitations which cannot be removed or reduced at acceptable cost. Distance to markets, and types of roads and farm structure are not taken into account in the assessment procedure. Reference must be made to the scheme for full details of the assumptions. Like the Canadian method, the British one has only seven classes. In particular, class 5 of the USDA method is excluded since it refers specifically to flat wet areas and thus breaks the theme of progressively greater limitations (Mackney, 1974). The American subclasses are also used with the addition of a subclass for gradient and soil pattern limitation. A distinctive characteristic of the British method is that classes are more precisely defined. As will be illustrated, actual limiting values for specific properties are specified. Climatic characteristics are incorporated in a quantitative manner in order to define three climatic groups. This is done on the basis of the water balance and temperature during the period April to September. In particular, figures for the following factors are obtained for this period:

R: average rainfall (in mm),
PT: average potential transpiration (in mm),
$T(x)$:   long-term average of mean daily maximum temperature.

Three climatic groups can thus be defined:

Group I
$$R - PT < 100 \text{ mm} \quad \text{and} \quad T(x) > 15 \,°C$$
(no, or only slight climatic limitations imposed on crop growth).

Group II
$$R - PT < 300 \text{ mm} \quad \text{and} \quad T(x) > 14 \,°C \text{ but excluding group I}$$
(moderately unfavourable climate which restricts choice of crops).

Group III
$$R - PT > 300 \text{ mm} \quad \text{or} \quad T(x) < 14 \,°C$$
(moderately severe to extremely severe climate which further limits the range of crops).

The Soil Survey of Scotland has further refined the assessment of climatic conditions by producing one map based on accumulated temperature and potential water deficit (Birse and Dry, 1970) and another on exposure and accumulated frost (Birse and Robertson, 1970).

The land use capability classes of the Soil Survey scheme can be summarised as follows:

Class 1. Land with very minor or no physical limitations to use.

Class 2. Land with minor limitations that reduce the choice of crops and interfere with cultivation.

Class 3. Land with moderate limitations that restrict the choice of crops and/or demand careful management.

Class 4. Land with moderately severe limitations that restrict the choice of crops and/or require very careful management practices.

Class 5. Land with severe limitations that restrict its use to pasture, forestry and recreation.

Class 6. Land with very severe limitations that restrict use to rough grazing, forestry and recreation.

Class 7. Land with extremely severe limitations that cannot be rectified.

(from Bibby and Mackney, 1969, pp. 3–4).

Since the publication of the scheme in 1969, the Soil Surveys of England and Wales, and Scotland, have been publishing land capability maps. For England and Wales, the more recent land capability maps are at the 1 : 25 000 scale whilst for Scotland, practically all published maps are at 1 : 63 360. An extract from a 1 : 63 360 Soil Survey map is shown in Fig. 2.3b. The area is located to the immediate west of Stirling in the Forth valley of central Scotland. The topographic extract (Fig. 2.3a) shows how the terrain ranges from the carselands to the Touch Hills to the south of Gargunnock. The soils range from poorly drained gleyed warp soils on the estuarine silts and clays to well and imperfectly drained brown forest soils on the lower valley slopes, to podzols and peaty podzols and to blanket peat which is most extensive on the uppermost areas. The caption to Fig. 2.3b shows how these soils are subdivided into associations and series. In Scotland a soil association refers to a group of topographically related soils developed on the same parent material. The Kippen Association, for example, includes a range of soils all derived from red sandstones with some yellow sandstones and schists. The land use capability map (Fig. 2.3c) reflects such soil variation with class 3 land on the carseland, classes 4 and 5 on the lower slopes, class 6 dominant in the peaty podzol and blanket peat areas on the upper and summit slopes and class 7 land restricted to very steep or very thin soil localities. The specific limitations vary from soil wetness and rooting zone limitations on the carselands, to slope and pattern limitations on the lower and middle slopes, to climatic and slope and pattern limitations on the highest land. The close association of topography, soils and land use capability class and subclass should thus be very evident for this area.

Despite the inclusion in the Bibby and Mackney (1969) scheme of critical values for defining selected characteristics, problems often are encountered in trying to assign sites to specific land capability classes. To aid this process, Burnham and McRae (1974) have produced a useful land-judging form which is reproduced in Appendix 2. At a site, the best possible class under A to V inclusive is recorded and then a search is made for the highest number, i.e. the lowest class. This provides the first approximation of land use capability class. The subclass symbols, w, s, g, c and e are given for the characteristics which result in the lowest class (maximum of two subclass symbols). The final step is to

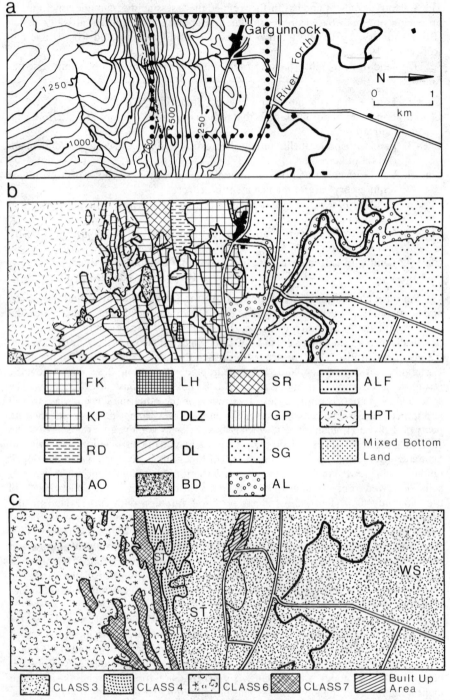

Fig. 2.3 Topography, soils and the land use capability of an area in the Forth valley in Scotland (see page 27 for the legend).

Figure 2.3a.   Topography in the vicinity of Gargunnock.
To the immediate west of Stirling in the Forth valley, Scotland: the square delimited by heavy dots corresponds to the area of mapped soils on Fig. 2.1. Contours are in feet (Extracted from Ordnance Survey 1:63 360 map, Sheet 54 Stirling)

Figure 2.3b.   Soils in the Gargunnock area

| Association | BROWN FOREST SOILS | | PODZOL | PEATY PODZOL | GLEY SOILS | |
	Freely drained	Imperfectly drained	Freely drained	Freely drained	Mineral poorly drained	Peaty poorly drained
Kippen	FK	KP	RD		AO	LH
Dalreith	DL			BD		
Sorn		GP			SR	

Other soils:
DLZ   Skeletal soil (Dalreith Association)
SG   Poorly drained gleyed warp soil (Stirling Association)
ALF   Alluvial fans
AL   Other recent alluvial deposits
HPT   Blanket peat

(Extracted from the 1:63 360 soil map produced by the Soil Survey of Scotland, Sheet 39 and part of 31, Stirling and Airdrie)

Figure 2.3c.   Land use capability in the Gargunnock area.
The classes are indicated by the types of shading; subclasses are shown by the following letters S (rooting zone limitations), W (wetness limitations), T (slope and pattern limitations) and C (climatic limitations) (Extracted from the 1:63 360 land use capability map produced by the Soil Survey of Scotland, Sheet 39 and part of 31, Stirling and Airdrie)

study the description of the determined class in Bibby and Mackney (1969) and decide if the result is reasonable – if not, some alteration to the first approximation is required.

This type of approach to classing of sites has been taken a further stage by Rudeforth and Bradley (1972). In a study of west and central Pembrokeshire, they obtained data from *c.* 1000 sites at the intersections of a 1 km grid. They converted the Bibby and Mackney (1969) scheme into a flow chart which thus permitted the design of a computer program. The merits of such an approach are clear – the taxonomic structure of the classification scheme has to be correct and the assignment of sites to classes becomes automatic once the data bank and program are complete. Rudeforth and Bradley (1972) found that a few modifications to the scheme had to be made. Rudeforth (1975) has developed this study by building in a greater degree of flexibility to the classification process. Figure 2.4 illustrates the generalised flow chart which was used to class soil and site data. As can be seen, six stages are involved (A to F). At stage C limits of properties acceptable to each class are set and after scanning the data for each site for each factor (identical to the approach in Burnham and McRae, 1974), modifications are made according to the degree of interaction between factors. The result in stage E is the allocation of sites to individual classes and such information can be plotted by computer. By analysing the soil and site as well as land use data, Rudeforth (1975) is able to

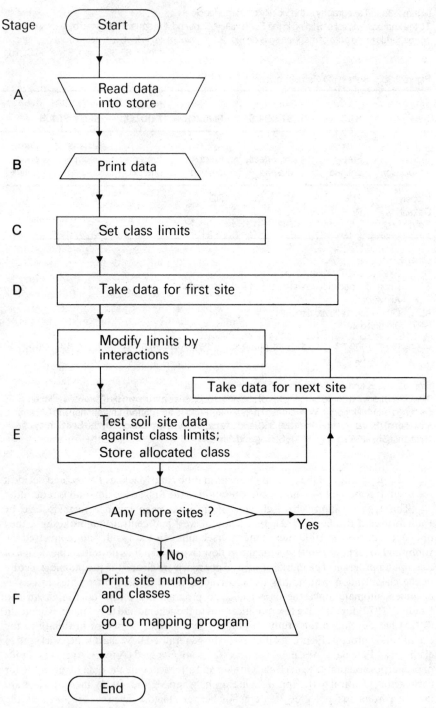

Fig. 2.4 Generalised flow chart for soil or land classing by computer (From Rudeforth, 1975, p. 157).

produce a series of maps showing actual and potential localities for such crops as barley and early potatoes. Rudeforth thus has adopted the land use capability scheme for a specific area and has utilised computer classing and mapping procedures. Davidson (1976b) in a study of terrain capability on sample farms used a computer program for classing sites in a manner similar to Rudeforth (1975).

Brief comment must be made on the application in Britain of land use capability maps to planning. As described in Chapter 1, account is taken of land capability in the zoning of land. For example, J. S. Bibby carried out a land capability survey of Mull, the results of which were incorporated into a *Comprehensive Development Report on Mull* (Highlands and Islands Development Board, 1971). The application of the land capability survey on Mull to development planning is discussed by Smith and Sutherland (1974). The survey indicated scope for developing agriculture and forestry. Another example is a study by Ormiston (1973) for the Highlands and Islands Development Board dealing with the Moray Firth area. For this investigation the Soil Survey of Scotland produced a land use capability map at the scale of 1 : 63 360. For general land use planning purposes, maps showing capability classes and subclasses seem thoroughly adequate, but levels of classification are not satisfactory at more detailed planning levels. For agricultural planning, subdivision of capability subclasses into units is necessary in order to identify land which can grow a similar range of crops, produce similar yields and which responds in a similar way to management and improvement practices. Hewgill (1977) demonstrates how a table listing the ratings of wetness and soil limitations as well as the land capability unit for each soil series for the Maltby sheet in Yorkshire is most useful for agricultural advisory work.

In this chapter we have examined the American, Canadian and British methods of land capability assessment. The close similarities between these approaches should be readily apparent. All the schemes resulted from a demand from planners, land users and conservation officers to provide non-technical information about the physical properties of land. The significance of land capability maps is beginning to be more widely appreciated. Issues concerned with land planning or management always tend to generate strong feelings, but in many countries there is the growing realisation that land resources are finite and are variable in quality and space. Bentley (1978) in his presidential address to the International Society of Soil Science, highlighted the limited reserves of good land in Canada as well as the loss of good agricultural land to urban development.

Mention was made in Chapter 1 of how the subject of land resources and their conservation has become a political issue in many states of the US. In Scotland, the Scottish National Party has suggested that there ought to be a land capability survey for the whole of Scotland. The indication is that demand will escalate for more specific quantitative data about the land resource base of countries and states. Thus schemes of land and soil assessment are being forced to evolve along more detailed and quantitative lines. The aim of the following chapter is to examine the developments in methodology and techniques during the 1970s.

CHAPTER 3
PRINCIPLES AND METHODS OF LAND ASSESSMENT

3.1 INTRODUCTION

In the previous chapters the major concerns were to demonstrate the relevance of soil information to land use planning, and to outline the methods of soil survey and soil assessment in terms of land use capability schemes. To a very large extent underlying principles associated with the evaluation process were ignored. Early in Chapter 2 a formal definition of soil was given, but it must have been apparent to the reader that the capability schemes used additional information to soil data. The Canadian scheme for wildlife capability clearly demonstrates this broadening of scope. Indeed, *soil* information is visualised as only one set of inputs in order to determine the *land* capability for a particular land use. Thus before attention is focused on the methodology of land evaluation, consideration must be given to the concept of *land*.

It is only possible to devise schemes of land evaluation or classification if the information to be assessed is precisely defined. The concept of land has been the subject of constant discussion since the first schemes of land classification were produced (Jacks, 1946; Kellogg, 1951). In fact land is interpreted in a wide variety of ways according to outlook. It can be viewed as embracing all the characteristics of the physical environment – the atmosphere, soil, geology, hydrology and flora and fauna. It may be considered as three-dimensional space within which man lives. Other interpretations take land as a consumer good or commodity, as location, as property or as a form of capital. An ecological view is also possible whereby land is equated with nature and is thus defined in terms of ecosystems. In the discussions convened by the FAO in 1972 concerned with developing a land evaluation framework, much consideration was given to defining land (Brinkman and Smyth, 1973). The ultimate definition which emerged from these FAO studies is worth full quotation:

'Land: an area of the earth's surface, the characteristics of which embrace all reasonably stable, or predictably cyclic, attributes of the biosphere vertically above and below this area including those of the atmosphere, the soil and underlying geology, the hydrology, the plant and animal populations, and the results of past and present human activity, to the extent that these attributes exert a significant influence on present and future uses of the land by man.'

(FAO, 1976, p. 67)

In essence land is thus viewed as *areas* composed of physical environmental characteristics which are or may be of importance to man's use of such areas. In a scientific sense this definition is far from satisfactory since an assessment of relevant characteristics is necessary before land can be defined. Thus two land evaluation researchers, for example, commissioned to investigate a particular area, could disagree from the beginning about the data which ought to be collected. Perhaps it is inappropriate to try to define in a scientific way *land*, though Moss (1978) suggests that a theoretical definition in terms of the function of land in the particular ecological system should ultimately be achieved. However, the FAO statement as quoted does provide clear guidance on how land can be interpreted.

3.2 EVALUATION METHODOLOGY

In a strict sense, to evaluate an area means to ascertain its extent or to express it in numerical form. Thus a soil or a geological map are particular kinds of evaluation. Often evaluation is taken to be synonymous with assessment which involves an estimation of value. So the objective of land evaluation or assessment is to judge the value of an area for defined purposes. The evaluation need not be limited to assessment of environmental characteristics, but the exercise can be extended to the point where the economic viability, the social consequences and the environmental impact of the proposals are also analysed. Thus the FAO (1976, pp. 1–2) proposes that a land evaluation project should be able to answer questions of the type:

How is the land currently managed, and what will happen if present practices remain unchanged?

What improvements in management practices, within the present use, are possible?

What other uses of land are physically possible and economically and socially relevant?

Which of these uses offer possibilities of sustained production or other benefits?

What adverse effects, physical, economic or social, are associated with each use?

What recurrent inputs are necessary to bring about the desired production and minimize the adverse effects?

What are the benefits of each form of use?

Various steps are necessary in order for the evaluation exercise to answer these types of questions. In the first instance there must be the clear statement on the objective of the study. As will be recalled, selection of relevant land characteristics (attributes of land which can be measured or estimated) is only possible within the context of a particular study. Two strategies are possible according to the *FAO Framework for Land Evaluation* (1976) once the objectives of a study are stated (Fig. 3.1). In the two-stage approach, an economic and social analysis may follow on from a qualitative land classification, whilst in the parallel approach the analysis of the land and land use relationships proceeds concurrently with economic and social analysis. Land use capability assessment is an example of the first stage of the two-stage approach, and, as demonstrated in Chapter 2, the results can be directly incorporated into planning decisions. Alternatively, the results of a capability assessment can be subjected to an economic and social analysis to provide a quantitative land classification which can be applied to planning. In essence the evaluation of land suitability means the assessment of land mapping units with respect to defined land uses which are physically, economically and socially appropriate to the area. An ecological basis to the evaluation methodology is thus clear – reflected in the approach of the *FAO Framework for Land Evaluation* (1976). Detailed studies which present an ecological methodology for land

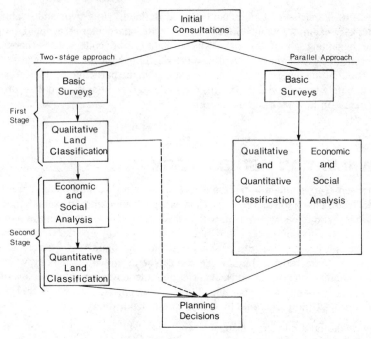

Fig. 3.1   Two-stage and parallel approaches to land evaluation (From FAO, 1976, p. 6).

evaluation are provided by Beek and Bennema (1972) and Beek (1978). In order to discuss such a methodology, consideration needs to be given to the use of various terms.

A distinction is made between a *major kind of land use* and a *land utilisation type*; the former is a major subdivision of rural land use, for example pasture land, forestry or recreation, whilst the latter is a type of land use described in greater detail (FAO, 1976). It must be stressed that land utilisation types are described not just in terms of actual land uses or crops, but also with reference to such factors as type of market orientation (subsistence or commercial production), capital intensity, labour intensity, technology employed, infrastructure requirements, size and configuration of land holdings, land tenure and income levels. An example of a land utilisation type as given in the *FAO Framework for Land Evaluation* (1976, p. 10) is:

> 'rainfed annual cropping based on groundnuts with subsistence maize, by smallholders with low capital resources, using cattle-drawn farm implements, with high labour intensity, on freehold farms of 5–10 ha.'

This example neatly demonstrates the type of information needed to describe a land utilisation type. It is also possible to have *multiple land utilisation types* (two different uses co-existing together, for example recreational uses within forestry areas), and *compound land utilisation types* (areas treated as one utilisation type though various forms of use may follow each other in sequence – a crop rotation, or different areas of land within the same functional unit – a mixed farm with both arable and pasture).

The task of detailed land evaluation is to assess land mapping units in terms of land utilisation types. This makes it necessary to recognise *land qualities* which are '. . . a component regime of the physical land conditions with a specific influence on land use performance' (Beek, 1977, p. 147). Four types of land qualities can be described (Beek and Bennema, 1972; FAO, 1976; Beek, 1978):

Land qualities related to:

1. *Plant growth* (for example, availability of water, nutrients, oxygen for root growth, etc.).
2. *Animal growth* (for example, hardships due to climate, endemic pests and diseases, nutritive value of grazing land, etc.).
3. *Forest growth* – natural or plantations (annual increments of timber species – influenced by many qualities listed under (1), pests and diseases, types and quantities of indigenous timber species, etc.).
4. *Management and inputs* (terrain factors affecting mechanisation, construction and maintenance of roads, size of potential management units, etc.).

Some of these qualities can be measured or estimated directly, but usually they have to be based on measurements of specific land characteristics – measures of such factors as slope value, soil depth, rainfall, etc. The distinction between land qualities and land characteristics can be demonstrated by considering erosional hazard. This problem is best assessed by analysis of the interaction of such factors as slope angle, slope length, rainfall intensity, soil permeability, etc. rather than by the individual assessment of these component characteristics. Thus the *FAO Framework for Land Evaluation* recommends that land units should be evaluated for land uses in terms of land qualities. To achieve such evaluation, *diagnostic criteria* are recognised; these may be land qualities or characteristics, but they are known to have a clear effect on land use output or potential. Critical values are associated with diagnostic criteria so that suitability classes can be defined. The *FAO Framework for Land Evaluation* considers the land quality 'oxygen available in the root zone' to demonstrate the nature of diagnostic criteria. In this case, soil mottling, soil drainage class or natural vegetation could be used as diagnostic criteria for assessing oxygen availability.

The preceding discussion underlines the importance of relating properties of land to land uses as an integral procedure of evaluation. Figure 3.1 outlines the steps involved in land evaluation, but gives no indication of the ecological foundation. To illustrate how land use considerations are incorporated into land evaluation methodology, the procedure as described in the *FAO Framework for Land Evaluation* (1976) is summarised (Fig. 3.2). The first step labelled 'Initial consultations' describes the preparatory work – a clear statement on the objectives of a study, the type of data to be used, the assumptions in the evaluation, the study area, the intensity and scale of the survey and the type of suitability classification to be used. At an early stage of the project the 'Kinds of land use' must be specified, though some modification of these may be necessary as the evaluation project proceeds. From a list of land uses considered relevant to the area, the required environmental conditions for each land use are determined. This may sound a straightforward task, but many difficulties are quickly encountered since detailed information on requirements of many land uses is inadequate. Practically all land evaluation projects require some type of physical resource survey – commonly a soil or soil–landform survey, and the results are presented in the cartographic form of 'Land mapping units' backed with appropriate analytical data. From this basic land inventory, 'Land qualities' can be postulated by a knowledge of the appropriate land use requirements and limitations. This 'Comparison of land use with land' is the key process in land evaluation since this is the crucial stage where the land and land use data, as well as economic and social information, are brought together and analysed.

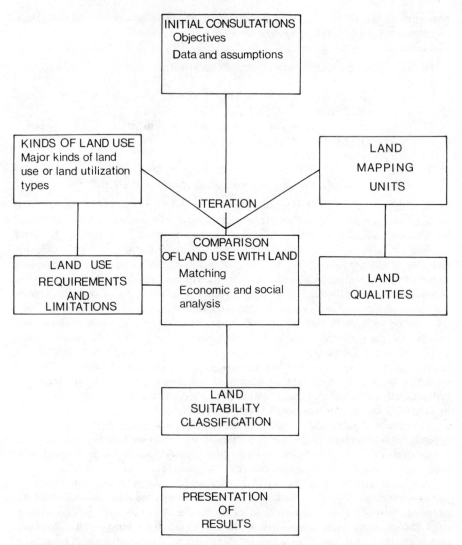

Fig. 3.2 Processes involved in land evaluation (From FAO, 1976, p. 28).

The results of this lead to the suitability classification. The term *matching* is used to describe the process in which the requirements of land uses are compared with land conditions in order to estimate or predict land use performance. Beek (1975) draws a distinction between qualitative and quantitative matching. With the former, a conversion table allows each land utilisation type to be graded in terms of degree of limitation posed by particular land characteristics. An example is given in Table 3.1 in which degrees of depth limitations are defined for four different land utilisation types. With quantitative matching, the assessment of land qualities is based on measured cause and effect relationships between the qualities and the land utilisation types. As indicated on Fig. 3.2, the comparison of land use with land may consist not only of matching, but also include economic and social analysis and perhaps a study of environmental impact.

Table 3.1   Guidelines for the interpretation of soil depth limitations for selected land utilization types (depth values in cm) (From FAO, 1975, p. 113).

LAND UTILISATION TYPE	DEGREE OF DEPTH LIMITATIONS				
	0	1	2	3	4
Cereals and pasture (rainfed)	+90	40–90	20–40	10–20	0–10
Annual root crops (rainfed)	+90	60–90	40–60	0–40	0–40
Deep-rooting perennials	+150	90–150	50–90	20–50	0–20
Irrigated farming	+150	100–150	50–90	20–50	0–20

On the basis of such comparison, a land suitability classification scheme can be defined which allows the presentation of results.

Figure 3.2 is a concise summary of the evaluation procedure, but in practice many difficulties are encountered. The methodology assumes that specific requirements of land uses or crops are known, but detailed information on the optimum growing conditions is often lacking. Information of the type illustrated in Table 3.1 is needed for a wide range of properties, but this is not usually available. This deficiency is increasingly being recognised. For example, Beek (1977) stresses the critical function of land qualities since they provide the link between land resource inventories and land use planning. The objective is to measure only the important land qualities so that they can be used to grade the land into the output or suitability classes appropriate to the land utilisation type. This is best achieved by a land quality/output analysis whereby the outputs in the form of yields, or soil erosional losses, for example, are correlated with land qualities. In order to carry out such statistical analysis, data from many field experiments are usually necessary.

The most difficult task in any land evaluation project occurs when data on land utilisation type and land mapping units are brought together in order to define a particular land suitability classification. At the level of reconnaissance investigations, such a problem is not too acute since the prime task is to eliminate areas clearly unsuitable to particular land utilisation types, but more detailed projects of land evaluation have to incorporate a more complex data analysis. Beek (1978), in describing this problem, proposes that a systems analysis is most appropriate in order to deal with the large number of variables.

The brief reference to a systems approach as applied to land evaluation brings discussion of methodology to the active research frontier. However, it should not be assumed that all exercises in land evaluation should adopt such an approach. Often the task is simply to provide a map showing specific problem areas for a particular land use. For example, a map showing areas with peat more than 1 m thick will be useful for the planning of constructional activity. Although the land use capability schemes as used, for example, in the US, Canada and Britain can be criticised on methodological grounds, the results from these schemes have been widely used for planning purposes. Thus it can be suggested that there will always be the need for comparatively simple, but broad schemes of land assessment for national or regional planning purposes, but at the local level, methods of analysis which can cope with the intricacy of many interrelated factors will become increasingly essential.

One aspect of this ecological approach to detailed land evaluation which seems understressed is the attitude of land users to their land. At the national or regional level there is need for the assessment of land with reference primarily to broad categories of land use; as described for the land use capability schemes, a moderately high level of management is assumed. As the level of analysis becomes more detailed, the methodology has increasingly to be able to incorporate the views of land users about their land. The problems associated with this can be exemplified by describing the results of a farm survey in north-east Scotland (Davidson, 1976b). The arable land on 81 sample farms was classified according to capability on the basis of soil and slope characteristics. A capability index was devised in order to express the overall capability for the arable area of each sample farm. Statistical analyses were then possible to establish if there was any relationship between farming type and capability, and between farmers' assessment of the grade of their land and its capability as determined by the survey. From a questionnaire survey it was found that farmers on better land were fairly divided in opinion about its quality whilst farmers with poorer land tended to have an over-optimistic view of its nature.

One way to interpret these results is to suggest that the scheme for capability assessment ought to have been varied according to the farming type. Thus the farms with the land of overall poor capability would have yielded much better grades if the assessment procedure had been carried out with specific reference to the rearing and feeding of cattle. On the other hand, these farms on more marginal land might be smaller, and the farmers less motivated to maximising their profits. Equally, their choice of farming type influences their view of their land; a farmer who concentrates on sheep and on the rearing of cattle will perceive his land in a different way to a farmer who rears and fattens cattle as well as growing a significant quantity of barley. This variable attitude to land characteristics can be demonstrated in the case of land slope. For instance a steep slope unit may be found to extend from one farm to an adjacent one and the respective farmers can display markedly different attitudes to the same slope. One might consider the slope too steep for regular ploughing and leave it in semi-permanent grass, whilst the other might not view the slope as providing any untoward danger and give it no special consideration in terms of land use. Such an example reveals the major difficulties involved in selecting slope values to define slope classes of relevance to more than one farmer. The conclusion to be drawn is that a very flexible methodological approach is required to land evaluation. At one extreme, national (and international) schemes are needed to assess land resources, but at the other, the ecological approach must be applied at the level of the individual management units. In the case of agriculture, there is need to develop Beek's (1978) systems approach to individual farms. As already indicated, this will only be possible if more data are available on the land requirements of particular land uses; equally there is need for research to investigate the ways by which farmers evaluate their own land.

3.3 THE FAO FRAMEWORK FOR LAND EVALUATION

Frequent reference has already been made to the *FAO Framework for Land Evaluation* (FAO, 1976: International Institute for Land Reclamation and Improvement, 1977). By the late 1960s most countries of the world had established their own particular systems of land evaluation and this obviously posed major problems for data exchange or collation on an international level. The idea was conceived in 1970 of an international consultation convened by FAO with the objective of developing a framework for land evaluation of application to the widest possible range of conditions. Various meetings took place and some of the material from these discussions has been published (Brinkman and Smyth, 1973; FAO, 1975).

Quite a number of the basic principles and methodology of the *Framework* have been described in section 3.2. It is worth stressing again that it is a framework rather than a fully defined classification method. In other words the *structure* of the evaluation procedure is described rather than the formal definition of specific classes. The *Framework* also places initial emphasis on the nature of the land use; as Beek (1978) puts it, in the *Framework*, the land utilisation type is the subject of land evaluation whilst the land unit is the object. Young and Goldsmith (1977) describe the *Framework* as resting on six basic principles. (1) Land is evaluated with respect to specific kinds of use (major kinds of land use or land utilisation types). (2) This evaluation requires a comparison of benefits with inputs, and (3) a multi-disciplinary approach. (4) The investigation is carried out within the context of nationally or regionally relevant conditions. (5) Any land use proposal if implemented must not result in severe or progressive degradation. (6) Results from a particular kind of land use must be compared with those from at least one alternative use.

The *Framework* describes a scheme for land suitability classification. The term *suitability* is used rather than *capability* to avoid any potential confusion with the American and other capability schemes. According to the *Framework for Land Evaluation* (1976) 'land suitability is the fitness of a given type of land for a defined use' (p. 17). Four levels of decreasing generalisation are defined:

1. *Land suitability orders:* reflecting kinds of suitability.
2. *Land suitability classes:* reflecting degrees of suitability within orders.
3. *Land suitability subclasses:* reflecting kinds of limitation, or main kinds of improvement measures required, within classes.
4. *Land suitability units:* reflecting minor differences in required management within subclasses.

(FAO, 1976, p. 17)

At the order level, an assessment is made as to whether the land is suitable or not for sustained use of the kind under consideration and yielding benefits which justify the inputs. Classes indicate the degree of suitability – up to a maximum of five, though three is common. Examples of classes are highly suitable (S1), moderately suitable (S2) and marginally suitable (S3). Subclasses indicate the type of limitation and are represented by lower-case letters, for example S2m for suitable land of class 2 with the specific limitation of moisture availability. The most detailed level in the classification structure is the unit. Units obviously are of the same class and subclass, but they vary in their production characteristics or in minor aspects of their management requirements. This level in the structure is designed to be applicable to individual farms. Units are indicated by arabic numbers, e.g. S2m – 1, S2m – 2, etc. Reference must be made to the *Framework* to obtain full details of the classification scheme. This brief outline combined with the principles and methodology as presented in section 3.2 means that the essential aspects of the *Framework* have been described. Before consideration is given to an example, it is instructive to summarise the types of information which the *Framework* suggests should be included in a land suitability report.

1. The context, in a physical, social and economic sense; background data and assumptions in approach.
2. Description of land utilisation types or of major kinds of land use.
3. Maps, tables and textual matter showing degrees of suitability of land mapping units for each kind of land use considered, together with the diagnostic criteria.
4. Management and improvement specifications for each land utilisation type with respect to each land mapping unit for which it is suitable.
5. Economic and social analysis of the consequences of the various kinds of land use considered.
6. The basic data and maps from which the evaluation was obtained.
7. Information on the reliability of the suitability estimates.

Since the *Framework* was only published in 1976, there are few studies to which it has been applied. The *Framework* gives some results from Brazil, Surinam and Kenya whilst Beek (1978) describes studies in Latin America. For present purposes it is instructive to summarise part of the investigation in the Central Region of Malaŵi by Young and Goldsmith (1977). They applied the *FAO Framework for Land Evaluation* to an area of 1 935 km² forming the greater part of the Dedza administrative district which lies within the moist savanna zone. Their first step was to define six major kinds of land use, viz. arable farming for annual crops, the cultivation of perennial (tree and shrub) crops, livestock production, two types of forestry (extraction from natural woodlands and forest plantations), and a combination of tourism with conservation. For these land uses, they then decided upon particular land qualities which affected land suitability. As an example, rooting properties were one land quality for arable farming of annual crops. The specific requirement is for deep soil of more than 150 cm and easy root penetration. Particular limitations occur with shallow soil or soil which roots find difficult to penetrate. Diagnostic criteria for such limitations are provided by measurements of effective depth and observations of particular texture/structure combinations. Having defined the relevant land qualities and surveyed the soil management units, the process of matching was possible whereby the requirements of the land uses were compared with the land qualities of the management units. As a result each unit is categorised at the land suitability class level of the *FAO Framework*, and in their paper Young and Goldsmith (1977) include a set of maps and a table illustrating the current suitability of soil management units for the major kinds of land use.

Integral to such an analysis is a consideration of potential environmental impact since steep slopes, for example, could suffer from a substantial erosion hazard if certain major changes in land use were to occur. Besides assessments of suitability for the six major land uses, evaluations are also made for individual annual crops such as different kinds of tobacco and potatoes. The method of presenting results in a matrix form in which the suitability classes for the major kinds of land use are specified for each soil management unit, allows the identification of *land use alternatives*. So far, the analysis has been *qualitative*, which, according to the FAO terminology, means that suitability classes have not been defined in common numerical terms, usually financial ones. As Beek (1978) notes, the distinction between qualitative and quantitative evaluations is blurred and he omits such separation. For example, a qualitative analysis rests on a firm data base – only the distinction between suitability classes is not made on a common numerical basis. Young and Goldsmith (1977), in pursuing this land suitability assessment, consider economic data in order to produce a quantitative evaluation.

At this more detailed scale of analysis, they define land utilisation types, for example nine different farming systems based on annual crops, but they relate these to the same soil management units as those of the qualitative study. A full description is given of the land utilisation types according to the *FAO Framework for Land Evaluation*, as well as an economic analysis to give figures of net income per hectare and per capita according to farming system and management level. This permitted a quantitative current suitability evaluation to be made in which, for specified management levels, net income per hectare and per capita were predicted according to land utilisation type and soil management unit. The results indicated that the greatest margins per hectare could come from mixed farming, annual crops with livestock, followed by forest plantations and arable farming without livestock. Coffee-growing indicates a loss, but Young and Goldsmith (1977) point out that such a result was based on 1975 coffee prices which have risen markedly making coffee-growing almost certainly profitable. The results of the quantitative economic analysis are added to the results of the qualitative evaluation so that land use alternatives can be suggested for each soil management unit. These alternatives are physically practicable, economically viable and environmentally sound. Such a statement of alternatives is the objective of land evaluation following the *FAO Framework for Land Evaluation*.

The study by Young and Goldsmith (1977) is particularly interesting, because not only is it amongst the first to use the *FAO Framework for Land Evaluation* but they carry out both a qualitative, mainly physical, and a quantitative, chiefly economic, analysis. Their reaction to economic analysis within land evaluation is one of caution since they recognise the short-term validity of such research. Prices and costs can quickly change thus invalidating results, and Young and Goldsmith (1977) also encountered difficulties in making assumptions about discount rates and shadow pricing. In conclusion they suggest that a clear distinction should be made between land evaluation and the economics of project appraisal.

3.4 SOIL INFORMATION SYSTEMS

The rise of soil information systems in the 1970s is another important development in soil science of relevance to land use planning. Credit must be given to the International Society of Soil Science which established a Working Group of Soil Information Systems; their first meeting was held in the Netherlands in 1975 (Bie, 1975), followed by meetings in Australia in 1976 (Moore and Bie, 1977), in Bulgaria in 1977 (Sadovski and Bie, 1978) and in Canada in 1978 during the 11th Congress of the International Society of Soil Science. In essence soil information systems result from the application of computers to the storage, processing and presentation of soil data. Several factors have combined to encourage the development of soil information systems. In recent years the necessary computer hardware and software to deal with maps and related spatial data has become available. Soil surveys generate an enormous amount of data so that computer-based storage systems are becoming increasingly essential. Information stored in this way can thus be used for a variety of purposes from soil classification to the automatic production of maps illustrating specific limitations for any defined land use. This demonstrates the flexibility in use of soil data which is possible with a soil information system, and, as noted in the preceding chapters, soil surveys are being approached increasingly to supply information for a wide variety of land uses.

The vital data input to a soil information system are soil profile descriptions supplemented with laboratory derived data. This is only possible with careful standardisation of field and laboratory techniques – field methods were described in Chapter 2. In Britain, for example, the *Soil survey field handbook* (Hodgson, 1974) has been the basis to a computer-based soil survey in a small area of southern Scotland (Ragg, 1977). Ragg used a portable tape-recorder for the collection of field data using a fixed-format record. The tapes were subsequently transcribed using the numerical codes of Hodgson (1974) to eighty column punch cards. Hazelden, Beckett and Jarvis (1976) successfully developed a proforma on which field observations could be directly coded, the advantage being to minimise the risk of error in transposition to cards or disc file. Systems are available which can translate coded profile descriptions to standard terminology, for example the Pedon Data System (Soil Conservation Service, USDA, 1973). The storage and easy retrieval of soil data from profile descriptions allows the first function of a soil information system to be achieved, viz. the determination of the properties of pedons.

Much work has been done on soil classification systems already and McCormack, Moore and Dumanski (1978) perceive that their development will be very much aided and made more efficient with computer storage of pedon properties. Such classification systems can be logically tested and applied to pedon data so that soil classification becomes automatic. This type of approach has been demonstrated for land use capability assessment by Rudeforth and Bradley (1972) and Haantjens and Bleeker (1975); in an Australian study, Armstrong and Wetherby (1977) have developed a computer-based procedure for the collation and analysis of soil data and they plan to use cluster analysis to select natural profile groups.

For land use planning, soil information systems can be of great assistance in making relevant soil data readily available. The output can be in tabular or cartographic form. For example, a farmer contemplating the improvement of some rough land might in the first instance approach a Soil Survey to establish if there was a profile description and analysis from such an area. A computer-based soil information system would allow quick recognition if such data were available and would be able to produce a printout indicating any particular nutrient deficiencies. If the soil information system also incorporated a file on crop yields in relation to soil characteristics, then the farmer could also be given data on the yields of different crops under various management strategies. Canada has developed one of the best soil information systems (called CanSIS) and integral to this system is a performance/management file. A longstanding problem in the application of soil survey to land use planning has been the time involved in the preparation and publication of soil maps. The production of such maps by computers will ultimately very much speed up the process, but such research is still at the experimental stage. A grid system is the easiest to apply to computer mapping with the resolution of the ultimate map being dependent upon the cell size. McCormack, Moore and Dumanski (1978) note that soil survey and land use data have been encoded for the entire State of Oklahoma and similar work is progressing in other states. The cells vary in size from about 4 ha to about 250 ha. Progress has also been made with polygonal systems which are capable of producing maps cartographically as good as conventional soil maps. An Advanced Mapping System has recently been applied in the US in which automatic scanning of conventionally produced soil maps is possible (McCormack, Moore and Dumanski, 1978). Such a development will very much speed up the publication of a soil map once the field survey is complete.

For land use planning, computer-generated interpretative soil maps are perhaps the most useful, a topic reviewed by Nichols and Bartelli (1974). As described above, a grid is first superimposed over a soil map and each cell is characterised according to dominant and possibly subdominant soil series. Nichols and Bartelli carried out an exercise of this type for Oklahoma County in Oklahoma using c. 16 ha cells. With such a data bank including information about individual soil series, it is possible to produce a wide variety of computer-generated maps. Nicholls and Bartelli demonstrate one such output with a map showing degree of limitations for the building of dwellings without basements. With soil data on a grid basis, it is also very easy to obtain tabular output giving, for example, total areas according to their suitabilities for different land uses. The merits of such an approach according to Nicholls and Bartelli are its versatility and its modest cost.

Another example to illustrate the application of a soil information system to land use planning can be taken from a project in New South Wales, Australia. There, the Soil Conservation Service were charged with executing a regional inventory and evaluation of land resources within the Bathurst–Orange growth area for the Development Corporation (Lynch and Emery, 1977; Hannam, Emery and Murphy, 1978). Other surveys are in progress for the shires of Goodradigbee, Yarrowlumla and Gunning, and for the Lower Hunter study. All these projects are dependent upon a soil information system and the methods are described by Lynch (1977). The principal objectives of the Bathurst–Orange study were to determine the extent and severity of soil erosion, and to classify the area according to agricultural and urban use capability. The data on soil erosion were required for the programme of soil erosion control whilst the land capability data were needed to assist with selecting the site for a new city and to ensure that the best agricultural land was retained for that purpose. The study area of 240 000 ha was gridded into cells of 16 ha. Aerial photo interpretation using photos at a scale of 1 : 32 000 permitted biophysical data on slope, terrain, land use and erosion to be collected for each of the 15 000 cells. The accuracy of the interpretation was checked by a field survey. The magnitude of the data necessitated a computer-based information system to be devised. All the information was punched on to computer cards and stored on magnetic tape with the locational and attribute data for each stored in one file. Data on the cells were maintained in sequential order to facilitate the production of line printer maps. Incorporated into the system were updating procedures whereby existing data on cells could be modified or new cells could be added. Information retrieved from the system can be in map and tabular form. Examples of line printer maps are given in Fig. 3.3 and 3.4. Both are taken from the Bathurst study by Hannam, Emery and Murphy (1978) and the computer maps were derived and compiled by L. Lynch. Figure 3.3 shows the variation in capability for agricultural purposes whilst Fig. 3.4 describes capability for urban areas.

The great advantage of such an information system is its flexibility – once the data bank is obtained, maps or tables for any specified purpose can be produced assuming that the relevant information is on file. This ease of access to soil or biophysical data should very much encourage planners to make increased use of this facility. One reason why planners have not made much use of soil information is because of its apparent difficulty of access and technical nature; soil information systems offer much scope for encouraging the use of soil data.

During the 1970s many countries have been developing soil information systems. In Europe, France and the Netherlands were the pioneers, though research has been initiated in almost all of the European countries (Garbouchev and Sadovski, 1978). As already mentioned, Canada with CanSIS has a sophisticated system (Dumanski, Kloosterman and Brandon, 1975). The underlying assumption to CanSIS is that soil data are essential for effective land evaluation and planning. The experience of CanSIS is that avenues of communication between soil scientists in the various provinces are improved (McCormack, Moore and Dumanski, 1978). In the US, work on the Resource and Management Information System by the Soil Conservation Service was started in 1976, though many independent systems had been used before then. In Australia, no

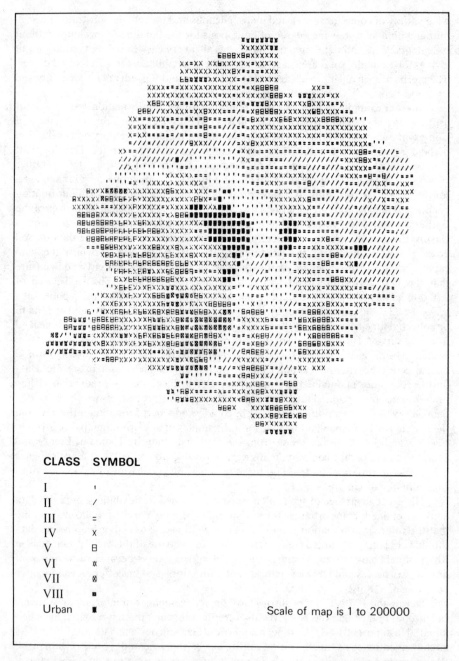

CLASS   SYMBOL

I	'
II	/
III	=
IV	X
V	⊟
VI	ⵕ
VII	ⵘ
VIII	▪
Urban	■

Scale of map is 1 to 200000

Fig. 3.3 A computer-produced map of agricultural capability for the Bathurst–Orange growth area in New South Wales, Australia. Classes I to III are suitable for cultivation, classes IV to VI for grazing, class VII for forestry and class VIII is unsuitable for any agricultural, grazing or forestry purpose (From Hannam, Emery and Murphy, 1978, map 7, by courtesy of L. Lynch).

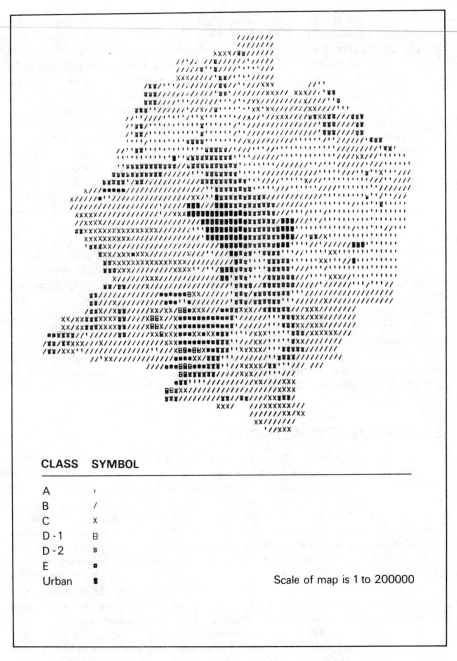

CLASS   SYMBOL

A   '
B   /
C   x
D - 1   ⊟
D - 2   ⋈
E   ▫
Urban   ∎   Scale of map is 1 to 200000

Fig. 3.4   A computer-produced map of urban capability for the Bathurst–Orange growth area in New South Wales, Australia. The classes indicate increasing difficulty posed by physical conditions to urban development (see section 4.3) (From Hannam, Emery and Murphy, 1978, map 8, by courtesy of L. Lynch).

integrated national system has yet been devised. At the international level, there is a move towards a soil data bank with the FAO as the organising body (Riquier, 1975; Riquier and Chidley, 1978). The publication of the *FAO–Unesco soil map of the world* combined with the production of guidelines by FAO on soil description and coding soil data make such an objective realistic. Riquier (1975) describes how the South America sheet of the *World soil map* has been digitised; besides soil information, data on climate, physiography, geology, vegetation, land use and land management have been recorded for each soil unit. Retrieval of between one and twenty single or associated land characteristics is then possible – areas with the specified characteristics can be shown on a television screen and then photographed. A soil data file is thus one of several in such an information system; Riquier (1975) also specifies files on location to permit automated cartography, results from fertilizer experiments, and on land use. A call for an international approach to soil information systems has also been made by Schelling and Bie (1978); they advocate the establishment by Unesco of an International Earth Science Data Centre, a centre not only to provide the services of an international soil information system but one also charged with the responsibility for research and the training of staff, especially from less developed countries. They argue that there is a very real need in an environmental sense for such an organisation; the technology is now available for computer terminals in any country to be linked via telecommunication networks thus negating the need for a large central data bank. The local terminal user would only need to transmit the data immediately required. Such developments may sound rather futuristic, but there are no technical reasons why such an international system could not be operational by the end of this century. However, it must always be remembered that soil information systems are dependent on basic soil surveys to produce the data base, and despite grandiose plans for international schemes there are still many parts of the world for which there is little soil information.

3.5 PARAMETRIC METHODS

The attraction of a method of land evaluation which is numerically based and avoids subjective assessment is obvious. According to Riquier (in FAO, 1974b, p. 74) as described by Beek (1978), parametric methods involve the selection of soil properties which are evaluated and awarded numerical scores; then these properties by means of the scores are substituted into mathematical formulae so that overall indices of suitability or performance are produced. The resultant values can be used themselves for assessment purposes, or alternatively they may be used to rank soils or to group soils into suitability classes. Before such methods are exemplified, the broader interpretation of the parametric approach by Mabbutt (1968) should be mentioned. He defines this '. . . approach as the division and classification of land on the basis of selected attribute values' (Mabbutt, 1968, p. 21). Thus, according to this view, any method of land evaluation involving the measurement of specific attributes is a parametric one. Speight (1968) has demonstrated the parametric approach in which values for such attributes as slope, rate of change of slope, contour curvature and unit catchment area can quantitatively describe landform elements. Soil, or land capability/suitability maps are derived from measurement of attributes and thus are results of a parametric approach according to Mabbutt's view. The identification of parametric methods in land evaluation unfortunately implies the existence of non-parametric methods. Modern techniques of land evaluation practically all involve measurement of attributes either directly or indirectly, and thus it seems more appropriate to accept the more limited interpretation of parametric methods; in particular, attention will be focused on some of the indices which have been used for assessing land.

An early index, designed to express soil quality, was proposed by Clarke (1951, 1971), and also summarised by Smith and Atkinson (1975). The method is based on three key field observations, viz. soil texture, depth and drainage. A soil pit is dug to a depth of at least 76 cm and for each horizon information on texture, depth and drainage is recorded. The overall profile value is obtained by multiplying a texture value (V) by a drainage factor (G), with the texture value being determined by multiplying the depth of each horizon (in inches) with a rating according to texture. For example a light loam (sandy loam) scores 16 and this would be multiplied by the depth of the horizon. Such results are added to give a texture value (V) which is then multiplied by the drainage factor (G) (again values are specified according to the depth at which gleying occurs) to give the profile value. The attraction of the method is its simplicity in being dependent on only three fundamental physical properties (Smith and Atkinson, 1975). Clarke (1951) shows that his profile values give a good indication of soil quality by establishing a close correlation between wheat yield and these values.

Another widely quoted early method is by Storie (1950, 1954), described for example by Olson (1974), Vink (1975) and Smith and Atkinson (1975). The 'Storie index' is obtained by multiplying scores for selected variables and the results have been applied in many studies, often after some modifications for local conditions. Olson (1974) selects the study by Nelson *et al.* (1963) on the island of Oahu in the Hawaiian group to demonstrate the approach. Another adaptation of the Storie method is provided by Leamy (1974b) who applied the technique in New Zealand. The framework of the New Zealand method can be summarised as follows:

Factor A: Rating based on the physical properties of the soil body
    1. Basal form
    2. Topsoil texture
Factor B: Rating based on the chemical properties of the soil body
    1. Plant nutrient status
    2. Soluble salt level
Factor C: Rating based on the nature of the environment
    1. Moisture regime
    2. Temperature regime
    3. Slope
    4. Erosion
    5. Microrelief
    6. Soil drainage
Factor D: Rating based on management

(From Leamy, 1974b, p. 9)

A percentage rating is calculated for each of these factors – the optimum and maximum figure obviously being 100. Leamy (1974b) specifies values for the various components of the factors. The overall soil index is obtained by multiplying the values of factors A, B, C and D; the final result is expressed as a percentage. Leamy (1974b) considers that such an index should prove to be very useful for farm valuation assessment.

Such an approach suggests that a general mathematical model is possible and Vink (1975, pp. 304–5) quotes one based on the work of Riquier (1972):

$$Y = 100 \times C \times Yp \times Ys \times Yv \times Yo \times Yt \times \ldots$$

where Y is yield in per cent of the maximum genetically possible for the variety specified under optimum conditions, C is the growth index of Papadakis (1952) corrected according to climate, soil and plant requirements, and Yp, Ys, Yv, Yo, Yt, etc. are the yields in per cent as a function of selected diagnostic criteria (for example, p = effective depth of soil, s = specific surface of soil, v = base saturation of soil, o = per cent organic matter content of soil, t = per cent salt content of soil, etc.).

The Storie index was developed primarily to assist with land assessment for taxation purposes in California. Other countries have also developed parametric methods of land assessment. Germany has had soil classification legislation since 1934, the aim being not only to ensure the fair assessment of taxes, but also to improve the basis for distributing grants and loans to agriculture, to assist in the planning of food production as well as the amalgamation and drainage of farms, and to provide a basis for land use planning and for agricultural advisory work (Weiers and Reid, 1974). The German land classification system is thorough and elaborate, and the result is that every hectare of non-urban land has been classified; Weiers and Reid in describing the German method, argue that such an approach is required in Britain given the need for a comprehensive, detailed and accurate land valuation scheme. For Eire, Lee (1977) proposes that the valuation of agricultural land should be based on the work of the National Soil Survey. An outline of the German method is given by Weiers (1975) with full details provided by Weiers and Reid (1974).

In the first instance the long-term use of each hectare of land is recorded and mapped. Then the actual nature of the soils is assessed according to whether the land is normally used for arable or grassland purposes. For full descriptions of the coding and rating schemes for soil, relief, climatic and general farm size and structure factors reference must be made to Weiers and Reid (1974). The result is an index figure for each hectare and these are then combined to produce a measure for every field since fields often exhibit variability in soil conditions. These measures on a field basis are combined to produce a soil–climate index for individual farms. The results for all farms in Germany are recorded in a real-estate register after an opportunity has been given for objections to the values. To achieve so-called standard valuations, the economic significance of the soil-climate index has to be determined.

The Clarke index, the Storie index and the German soil–climate index are all illustrations of parametric techniques according to the definition accepted earlier in this section. Specific data for these methods need to be collected, tables consulted and formulae calculated in order to produce the results which are tested in terms of usefulness by reference to yield figures for particular crops, gross margins of farms or market value of farms. By way of conclusion to this section on parametric methods, it should be pointed out that there is a considerable body of research which has examined the relationships between soil or land types and agricultural yields in biological or economic terms. For example, Fenton *et al.* (1971) have carried out extensive research in Iowa relating crop yields of corn, soybeans, oats and hay to 290 selected soil types and phases. Such a study aids the interpretation of soil survey work as well as providing a basis for rating soils. In a more recent paper, Fenton (1975) describes how each soil mapping unit in Iowa is assigned a corn suitability rating based on relationships between corn yields and benchmark soils. The ratings also take into account local climate and soil erosion risk, as well as some other specific considerations. The results are shown to produce an equitable assessment of agricultural land for taxation purposes. Similar consistency and equitability in evaluating rural land are demonstrated for Illinois in a study by Mausel, Runge and Carmer (1975). However, a study in Northern Ireland by Cruickshank and Armstrong (1971) has indicated that caution needs to be exerted before morphologically based soil maps are used for agricultural land classification. By multiple regression analysis, they relate gross margins of farms and crops and livestock to specific soil variables. The varying relationships suggest that individual soil maps are needed for each farm enterprise, with the criteria of mapping being the relevant soil properties as determined by the regression analysis. Again, the importance of establishing a statistical relationship between soil properties and return from the land is evident. It is also possible to develop models for predicting yield from studies relating capability classes and economic returns (e.g. Patterson and Mackintosh, 1976) or between agroclimates, capability classes and economic returns (e.g. Peters, 1977).

3.6 THE LAND SYSTEM METHOD

This approach was used as far back as 1933 in Michigan (Cooke and Doornkamp, 1974), but credit is usually given to the Commonwealth Scientific and Industrial Research Organisation (CSIRO) in Australia for pioneering the technique in the 1940s to assess the agricultural and pastoral potential of northern Australia. A rapid method for describing, classifying and mapping large areas was required. The first area to be mapped was the Katherine–Darwin region in 1946 and this study by Christian and Stewart (1952) has come to be the model for many others. Since this first survey, about 2 million square kilometres of Australia and most of Papua New Guinea have been covered.

The land system approach, also called integrated survey, is fully described by Christian and Stewart (1968); outlines of the technique are also given by Cooke and Doornkamp (1974), Mitchell (1973), Vink (1975) and Young (1976). King (1970) describes how a parametric approach can be applied to land system classification. Thomas (1976) provides a review of land resource surveys. To a very large extent this method is based on the interpretation of aerial photographs and areas with a recurring pattern of topography, soils and vegetation are mapped as individual land systems. The central concept is that in specific areas all the environmental characteristics (topography, soils, vegetation, geology and geomorphology and climate) will interrelate, resulting in distinctive patterns on aerial photographs. The approach is described as integrated because the method depends on identifying distinctive areas resultant upon the integration of environmental variables; the survey is also executed by a team of scientists (for example, a geomorphologist, geologist, pedologist, ecologist and an agriculturalist). The resultant maps showing the distribution of land system are produced on scales varying from 1 : 250 000 to 1 : 1 000 000 and it can be recognised immediately that the land system approach is essentially a reconnaissance assessment of natural resources. For the planning of agricultural development, such surveys are able to identify areas of little or no potential, but more detailed investigations are required in areas which seem to offer scope for development.

A report on an area which has been surveyed by the land system approach contains not only a land system map, but also other maps, for example of geology or geomorphology; the properties of individual land system are summarised in tables giving information on the geology, topography, major soils, major vegetation communities, characteristics of agricultural importance and comments on agricultural potentialities. The nature of the land system is also illustrated by the presentation of a schematised block diagram for each one. Such diagrams and tables permit the description of the components of land system, viz. land units which clearly display a greater deal of internal homogeneity than land system.

Organisations other than CSIRO have also applied the land system approach to land resource assessment. The Land Resources Division of the Ministry of Overseas Development undertake such surveys as part of the British foreign aid or under contract. Young (1978) summarises the research of this unit. Projects involving a land system analysis have been carried out in such countries as Lesotho (Bawden and Carroll, 1968), north-east Nigeria (Bawden, Carroll and Tuley, 1972), Zambia (Mansfield *et al.*, 1975–76), and Ethiopia (King and Birchall, 1975). These surveys are very much of a reconnaissance nature; where the need is for more detailed land resource assessment, recourse is made to soil survey procedures (Ch. 2). This soil data, combined with vegetational and climatic information, allows land use capability maps to be produced. For example in the Belize study (Jenkin *et al.*, 1976), land is classed as to whether it is suitable for arable use (further subdivided into four classes), conditionally suitable for arable land (further subdivided into two classes), and unsuitable for arable use (further subdivided into two classes). The results are presented on maps at a scale of 1 : 100 000.

Reference must also be made to research on terrain classification and evaluation by an Oxford team (Webster and Beckett, 1970). This work was sponsored in the first instance by the Military Engineering Experimental Establishment (MEXE), now the Military Vehicles Experimental Establishment (MVEE), since the military need was for the development of a fast method which could predict the trafficability of terrain for army vehicles. The method focused on the identification and mapping from aerial photographs of land facets at scales of 1 : 10 000 to 1 : 50 000. A facet '. . . is a part of the landscape, usually with simple form, on a particular rock or superficial deposit, and with soil and water regime that are either uniform over the whole of the facet or if not, vary in a simple and consistent way' (Webster and Beckett, 1970, p. 54). Land facets are grouped together to produce land systems which are mapped at scales in the range 1 : 250 000 to 1 : 1 000 000. The close similarity between the CSIRO and MEXE land system as well as between the respective land units and land facets should be immediately clear. The particular contribution which the Oxford team made was to carry out field trials of their method to see whether the technique would permit the classification of all the terrain in the area, to test if the mapped facets were internally homogeneous in terms of specific variables, and to test whether different photo interpreters would produce similar results. Overall, the outcome of this investigation was satisfactory which led the Oxford method to be applied in surveys in such countries as Uganda, Swaziland, Kenya and parts of southern Africa. King (1975) has also carried out research to determine if land systems can be investigated in a quantitative manner. He established by statistical analysis a large number of correlations between geomorphic, soil and land system data for an area in Zambia. A recent study has investigated whether the land system–facet classification could be applied in the Western Highlands of Scotland, and if so, whether the results could provide a basis for the acquisition of information on soil and land capability (Lawrance *et al.*, 1977). The general approach proved to be applicable, though land facets were found to be rather complex and had to be subdivided into land elements. The method has also been used as a basis for providing information for a data bank to speed up the process of terrain evaluation (Beckett *et al.*, 1972).

Without doubt there has been much improvement in land resource surveys using the land system approach since the pioneering work in the 1940s and 1950s. A distinct trend has been towards making aerial photo interpretation more objective through the use of more sophisticated remote sensing techniques and through being more specific about relevant land attributes. Nevertheless, some fundamental objections are still voiced about the method. For example, Moss (1978) argues that such land resource reports contain much data of dubious or irrelevant value through trying to describe so many characteristics. This criticism may well be valid for the older surveys, but more recent investigations seem to have more particular objectives and are thus more specific in approach. These themes can be illustrated by outlining studies in Malaysia and Mauritius which have used the land system approach.

The study in Malaysia exemplifies the Oxford method as applied to terrain evaluation for highway engineering (Lawrance 1972, 1978). This project, carried out by the Overseas Unit of the Transport and Road Research Laboratory, had the objectives of testing the Oxford method in a humid tropical environment and of examining the variability of soil properties of relevance to engineering within mapped units. A map at a scale of 1 : 250 000 shows the distribution of land systems within the study area; the accompanying report contains information in tabular form about the component land facets. Attention is focused on their topography and the nature of their soils from an engineering standpoint. In particular, information is given according to the British soil classification system for engineering purposes. Block diagrams, topographic sections and annotated stereo triplets indicate the spatial pattern of land facets within land systems. By describing the problems of an engineer working in an unfamiliar area, Lawrance (1978, p. 3) illustrates the use and advantages of the land system approach to terrain classification:

'An engineer is to supervise the regravelling and the maintenance of a gravel road, in an area known to him only superficially. He traces the line of the road on the land system map, and notes that it lies within one land system. He turns up the land system by name in the report, and finds under the description of the land facets that a lateritic soil profile typically occurs on the crests of low hills, and at the change of slope between these and steep hills. The low hills are labelled facet 2, and are distinct on the aerial photographs from the higher, steeper hills (facet 1) and broad flat valleys (facet 3), neither of which have lateritic soil profiles ascribed to them. He identifies on aerial photographs the three land facets which recur along the length of the route, taking particular note of hill crest sites which occur near the road line, where gravel is most likely to be found. In the field he travels from one low interfluve crest to the next, placing only one or two pits on each to establish the nature of the material. Although the laterite is by no means always well developed, at the end of the survey he finds half a dozen sites containing good quality material, which are then surveyed in detail for their quantity.

'The intensive survey reveals that laterite deposits found on interfluves at the base of the steeper hills are more abundant and of better quality than those found on crests in the absence of a steep hill above. This piece of information, together with a summary of the grading, plasticity and strength tests made on the chosen gravels are noted in a small filing system kept in the provincial office, indexed under the heading of that land facet in that land system. These data can be retrieved in a few minutes when information is required about laterite gravels in the area.'

This hypothetical situation as described by Lawrance clearly indicates how such an engineer in the early stages of a project could benefit from the results of a land system analysis. However, it should not be assumed that such information would be used by engineers if it was available. A study of engineering site investigations in Scotland, for example, indicates many weaknesses, one of which was the general lack of knowledge about relevant information contained in published soil and geological maps with their associated reports (Matheson and Keir, 1978). Nevertheless, the investigation by Lawrance (1972, 1978) negates Moss's (1978) criticisms of the land system approach through illustrating a purposive terrain analysis resulting in measured values of direct relevance to particular land uses.

The Malaysian example shows how the land system approach can provide specific data, and the example from Mauritius illustrates how this approach can be applied at a detailed level to assist land use planning. The particular interest of the Mauritius study lies in the fact that the CSIRO approach has been applied at the land unit and complex level in order to assess land suitability using the FAO method. The results of the land resource and agricultural suitability evaluation of Mauritius were compiled by Arlidge (1973), and an accompanying report has also been written by Arlidge and Cheong (1975).

The basis of the resource survey was the interpretation of aerial photographs (scale 1 : 15 000) by pattern analysis, the assumption being that pattern variations on the photographs correlated with certain soil conditions, expressed through differences in landform, drainage, erosion and vegetation features. The aim was to identify and map land units, parts of the land surface over which the physical characteristics were considered relatively uniform. These land units were also grouped into particular land complexes, the term 'complex' being used in preference to 'system'. The resultant maps are published at a scale of 1 : 50 000 and show the distribution of thirteen land complexes which are made up of forty-four land units. Descriptions are given in the report of the land complexes and units.

These units were then evaluated following the FAO method in terms of their suitability with respect to seven land utilisation types, viz. (1) sugar-cane, (2) food crops, (3) mixed cropping, (4) paddy rice, (5) tea, (6) productive forestry and/or livestock fodder or grazing, and (7) protective forestry, wildlife and recreation. Following the specification and rating of appropriate land qualities for each of the seven land utilisation types, a land suitability classification was evolved. The legend on the map gives the suitability ratings for the land utilisation types after specified major improvements have been completed. The document accompanying the maps (Arlidge, 1973) gives a suitability assessment to the subclass level (see section 3.3) of the forty-four land units for seven land utilisation types.

It can be readily appreciated from this brief summary that the Mauritius project ably demonstrates how the CSIRO land system approach can be developed to produce detailed results of obvious relevance to land use planning. As already stated, the particular importance of the Mauritius study is how it builds a suitability assessment using the FAO approach upon a land resource survey based on the CSIRO method.

To conclude this review of the principles and methods of land assessment, it is important to identify a current trend towards more ecological approaches. To a large extent this should have been evident from the discussion in sections 3.2 and 3.3 when the nature of the *FAO Framework for Land Evaluation* was outlined, since its entire approach is ecological. An analysis following this method starts with specified land uses, considers the relevant land qualities conducive to land use success, and then proceeds with assessing the mapped units with reference to the appropriate properties. The land system approach can also be described as ecological since areas are mapped on the basis of patterns resultant upon the interaction of physical characteristics; Vink (1975) visualises an integrated survey as being ecologically based. Moss (1968 a, b and c; 1978) has been a strong advocate of an ecological approach to land classification, but credit must also be given to G. A. Hills who has done pioneering work in Canada since the early 1950s though it is only in recent years that he has developed an integrated approach to ecosystem classification (Hills, 1976). Indeed, it seems as though Canada is in the forefront with an ecological approach to land classification, reflected in the existence of a Canada Committee on Ecological (Biophysical) Land Classification (Thie and Ironside, 1976; Wiken and Ironside, 1977). The Canadian work can be exemplified by brief consideration of one investigation.

A study entitled *An Ecological Input to Regional Planning* has been carried out by Coleman (1975) for the regional municipality of Waterloo, an area of 1 336 km² located about 95 km to the west of Toronto. Coleman argues that the role of ecological analysis in regional planning is to provide information on the environmental implications of alternative plans. He developed a computer-based data bank on biophysical attributes (geology, climate, soil, land use and vegetation). The use of computer mapping techniques allowed him to produce a large number of maps, for example maps of soil drainage, slope class, different land uses, gravel resources, frost hazard, engineering soil groups, and soil capability for residential development and for many other land uses including golf course fairways.

The study by Coleman very neatly illustrates many of the trends in methods of land assessment as discussed in this chapter, viz. the ecological approach where the landscape is approached as a functional entity, the tendency towards computer-based systems of data storage and retrieval, the swing away from rather generalised assessments of land towards more specific ones for defined land uses or land use activities, and the emphasis on quantitative methods so that not only are land attributes measured but quantitative predictions about land yield or performance are produced.

CHAPTER 4
SOIL ASSESSMENT FOR PARTICULAR PURPOSES

4.1 INTRODUCTION

As discussed in Chapter 2, the USDA method of land use capability is relevant to a range of land uses. As the degree of limitation increases, then the number of land use options decreases (Fig. 2.2). In the Canada Land Inventory schemes, land use capability is separately assessed for a number of land uses, viz. agriculture, forestry, recreation, ungulates and waterfowl. Quite obviously the criteria for defining the component capability classes vary according to the type of land use. The trend towards assessment procedures geared to particular land uses is further demonstrated by the *FAO Framework for Land Evaluation* (FAO, 1976) in which the starting point is the land use. The *Framework for Land Evaluation* provides a structure by which land can be evaluated for any defined purpose as long as the land use requirements are known and the necessary data about land are available. The Mauritius study as described in section 3.6 illustrates how the island was evaluated using the FAO approach for seven different land utilisation types. The trend towards specific, detailed and quantitatively based land evaluation projects is thus very evident. In this chapter attention is given to particular methods of soil assessment which have been used for the planning of irrigation schemes, urban areas and recreational areas. However, this should not detract from the fact that the dominant purpose of soil assessment for land use planning is to aid agricultural planning and management. The principles and methods discussed in the preceding chapter are largely geared towards agricultural needs.

Of course forestry can be treated in the same way with evaluation schemes designed to give information on the suitability or yields of particular soils or land types in relation to tree species. In Britain, one of the first tasks which the Forestry Commission undertakes when they acquire new land is to carry out a survey of the physical conditions so that the most appropriate species are planted. An example is provided by Paterson and Webster (1977) who describe the use of soil mapping for forestry purposes in the North York Moors. According to Toleman (1974), the most relevant factors to be included in a land classification for forestry are:

altitude	accumulated growing season temperature
soil type	winter coldness
windiness	precipitation surplus
aspect	potential water deficit in the growing season
topographic class	pollution
slope	
vegetation type	

The importance of these factors varies according to the species, though Toleman (1974) reports pilot results from investigations in Scotland which suggest that soil type is the most important variable in influencing forest yield. He is able to produce tables which predict for Scotland average forest yield according to broad site types (soil group, elevation and general location). Guidance on a more qualitative basis is provided by Pyatt, Harrison and Ford (1969) for north and mid-Wales on the significance of soil types for forests. In Britain no capability scheme has been developed similar to the forestry scheme of the Canada Land Inventory.

More numerically based methods are also being applied and two approaches can be identified. The first involves computer-based methods for assigning soils to suitability classes relevant to tree species. Such an approach is demonstrated by Bie *et al.* (1976) for the species ash. The second approach is parametric in which indices are calculated after several environmental variables are measured. For example, in central Japan, Mashimo (1974) has related an index of growth for the tree species *sugi* to nine variables (altitude, topographical position, aspect, soil type, thickness of A horizon, organic content of soil, soil texture and stoniness and hardness of soil). The multiple correlation coefficient between all these variables and the site growth index was very high (0.963) whilst the soil type variable produced the strongest partial correlation coefficient (0.789), a general result also obtained by Toleman (1974) for Scotland. However, the effect of soil type on tree growth is not always so evident. In the Missouri Ozarks, for example, Watt and Newhouse (1973) were unable to establish statistically differences in the growth of oaks between soil phases. The study by Watt and Newhouse indicates the problems which can arise when a soil classification developed for agricultural purposes is applied to silviculture. The need seems to be for more studies using experimental plots in order to examine the relationships between measures of tree growth and soil, topographic and climatic characteristics. Results of the type achieved by Mashimo (1974) can then be the basis of parametric methods for the quantitative assessment of soils with reference to tree species.

4.2 SOIL ASSESSMENT FOR IRRIGATION

About one-third of the world's land surface suffers from a moisture deficiency which presents a major constraint to agricultural development (Zonn, 1977). Any significant increase in agricultural output from arid and semi-arid regions is dependent upon new irrigation schemes. Such projects are highly expensive and necessitate very careful planning to ensure ultimate economic and social success. Bergmann and Boussard (1976) provide a *Guide to the Economic Evaluation of Irrigation Projects*. They identify four stages in the planning process prior to actual construction and these are listed below:

1. Outline survey

This is an initial survey to provide a rough outline of the project by discussing it with hydrologists, soil surveyors and agricultural officers, all familiar with the study area.

2. Preliminary project

Reconnaissance field surveys of pedological, hydrological, topographical and geological conditions are carried out to assess the environmental feasibility of the proposed scheme.

3. Feasibility report

The results from the previous stage permit an analysis of the proposed project including an economic evaluation. The first estimates of returns on overall investment should become available. Also, estimates are made of the economic viability of farms which will be established on completion of the irrigation scheme.

4. Definitive project

The detailed survey work and resultant planning are only undertaken if the results from stage 3 are favourable. In stage 4, topographical, pedological, geological, climatological and hydrological conditions are investigated in detail. Such data combined with information on costs of construction of the scheme including new roads, farms, etc. as well as estimates of crop returns, allow a thorough economic appraisal of the project. If the project is to proceed, then the data collected during the definitive project stage are also used for the detailed planning of the project.

These stages are described to illustrate how the planning of irrigation projects requires an integrated approach; soil survey work is only one type of input to the planning process. It can also be seen that such soil information is required at varying levels of detail ranging from introductory qualitative assessments at stage 1 to intensive field sampling combined with the laboratory determination of many soil properties at stage 4. The definitive text on irrigation is provided by Hagan, Haise and Edminster (1967) and Hudson (1975) gives a succinct introduction from the engineering standpoint.

Soil survey work is necessary not only at various stages of an investigation for an irrigation project, but also for different purposes. New crops are usually grown in an area following the installation of an irrigation scheme, and thus soils must be assessed in terms of their suitability for these crops. Soil types also influence the methods of irrigation. For example, soils with a high storage capacity can be irrigated with large quantities of water infrequently (for example, flood irrigation), whilst soils with a high rate of infiltration have to be irrigated frequently, but with small quantities (for example, by sprinkler methods). Soil surveyors, besides describing soil types before irrigation, have to predict the effect of irrigation on soil characteristics since many physical, chemical and biological changes may be induced. Maletic and Hutchings (1967) postulate possible changes in soil structure through modification of salinity level, an increase in exchangeable sodium, a change in organic matter content and alteration of clay minerals. The marked increase in the downward movement of water may result in the translocation of clay ultimately producing an argillic horizon which will impede the movement of water. Changes in cation exchange capacity as well as in the amounts of such salts as calcium sulphate and calcium carbonate may also occur. Information on the quality of the applied water is also essential since such water, if it contains a high suspended or chemical load, will influence the soil. Emphasis is given in this section to the methods of soil assessment which are used to aid the selection of areas suitable for irrigation.

The principles and methods of selecting and classifying land for irrigation are discussed by Maletic and Hutchings (1967). In particular, they examine the physical factors appropriate to this topic under the headings of climate, soil, topography and drainage. In terms of soils, it is possible to list the following field observations and laboratory analyses particularly relevant to irrigability:

1. Field observations

Texture; depth to bedrock, hardpan, sand, gravel, caliche or other root zone limitation; structure; consistence; colour; mottling; kind and sequence of horizons; drainage conditions; depth to water table.

2. Field tests

Infiltration rate/hydraulic conductivity.

3. Laboratory tests

Particle size distribution; bulk density; porosity; clay mineralogy; surface area; availability of nutrients including exchangeable sodium; cation exchange capacity; base saturation; electrical conductivity; hydraulic conductivity; pH; sulphate and carbonate content; organic matter content; soil moisture retention and available water; measure of structural stability; effect of leaching on salt content.

(Based on Maletic and Hutchings, 1967, pp. 133–4)

It can be readily appreciated that it is rare for all these observations and tests to be executed; the level of detail required in an investigation would depend upon the stage of the analysis and the amount of money available to fund laboratory testing. The task of soil assessment is to evaluate the results of these observations and tests in terms of suitability for irrigation. The significance of particular soil attributes will vary according to such issues as the natural climatic regime, the method and rate of irrigation, the types of proposed crops and how they are managed, and the availability of finance to overcome any particular soil problem. For guidance, Maletic and Hutchings (1967, p. 135) give advice on soils suitable for sustained irrigation in the western USA. These soils are permeable and have field-measured hydraulic conductivities ranging from about 1.27 to 127 mm/hr, textures ranging from loamy sand to friable clay, cation exchange capacities more than 3 meq/100 g, depths to root limiting influences varying from 30.5 cm to 152.4 cm or more, water-holding capacities varying from 6.25 to 25.00 cm/m, salinity levels at equilibrium with the irrigation water at 8 mmhos/cm or less, and exchangeable sodium not more than 15 per cent. In addition the level of the water table must be maintained naturally or artificially at such a depth to prevent oxygen deficits and the accumulation of soluble salts or exchangeable sodium within the rooting zone of plants. The soil requirements are reproduced in order to demonstrate properties and values considered significant for assessing the irrigability of soils in the western USA. As already stated, these requirements must be varied according to area and proposed crops; for example soils with cation exchange capacities less than 3 meq/100 g may produce good yields under irrigation in the tropics and crops also vary in their tolerances to saline conditions (Maletic and Hutchings, 1967).

Description and the intensive sampling of soils followed by many laboratory analyses are normal for stage 4 (the definitive project) in the planning process of irrigation schemes. The need at stage 2 (the preliminary project) is to carry out a rapid assessment of soils in terms of their irrigability. If the area has been mapped by standard soil survey, then careful examination of the mapping units may suggest those particularly suitable or unsuitable for irrigation. The essential problems are that routine soil survey does not produce all the data for assessing the irrigability of soils, and in addition the boundaries of soil mapping units may not coincide with boundaries corresponding to differences in soil suitability for irrigation. However, a soil survey carried out by standard techniques, but geared towards the needs of an irrigation project, can produce useful results. A description of a soil survey and irrigability classification scheme in a particular study should aid comprehension.

The selected project is an investigation of an area of *c.* 1 020 ha proposed for irrigation to the immediate east of Lusaka in Zambia (Yager, Lee and Perfect, 1967). The soils of the area were surveyed by routine methods resulting in a map showing the distribution of soil series and soil phases. Then each of these soils was assessed with reference to an irrigability classification which was designed to represent a simple and general evaluation of soil and slope factors related to the ability to produce crops under irrigation. The prime factors seem to have been slope, soil depth, texture, permeability, drainage, water-holding capacity and infiltration rate. Six classes were then defined though no occurrence of the grades 1 and 5 were found. Class 2 was described as moderately good, class 3 as fairly good, class 4 as not irrigable except under special conditions, no description was given of class 5 whilst class 6 was land unsuitable for irrigation due to shallow depth. The classes were further subdivided according to specific limitations with the letter **t** indicating a slope difficulty, **d** a wetness limitation and **s** a difficulty resultant upon the sandy nature of upper horizons. The results of the investigation are shown on Fig. 4.1; the solid lines indicate the boundaries between the original soil series and phases which have been interpreted using the irrigability classification. The accompanying report by Yager, Lee and Perfect (1967) gives information on the mapping units to justify their assignments to the irrigability classes. The size of the proposed dam combined with the evaporation rate allowed the estimation that *c.* 280 ha could be irrigated; Yager, Lee and Pefect (1967) state that the class 2 soils are the most suitable to receive such water though they stress that more detailed investigations will be necessary to aid the design of the actual irrigation scheme.

A number of studies could have been selected to illustrate this approach whereby soil mapping units are interpreted in terms of their suitability for irrigation. For example, a detailed investigation has been carried out by Maker, Downs and Anderson (1972) for Sierra County in New Mexico. In this study, not only are the eighteen soil associations evaluated with respect to irrigation, but also with regard to suitability for engineering purposes. It should also be noted that projects concerned with assessing soils for irrigation are not limited to those parts of the world with a very distinct dry season. For example, the soils in the Müstair valley in Switzerland have been investigated with the specific objective of identifying areas particularly suitable for irrigation (Peyer *et al.*, 1976).

As with land use capability or suitability schemes, there is much advantage if one particular framework proves applicable to a wide range of studies concerned with land and irrigation. The system developed by the United States Bureau of Reclamation (USBR) for their irrigation development schemes in the US has been applied in many other countries, often after certain modifications. Details of this scheme are provided by the Bureau of Reclamation (1953) and Maletic and Hutchings (1967), Olson (1974), Hudson (1975) and Vink (1975) give summaries. It needs to be stressed that the USBR scheme is not only concerned with soil conditions but with all the factors which influence the ultimate financial returns from an area once an irrigation scheme is installed. In fact the scheme defines land classes according to the relative degree of *payment capacity* which is the amount of money left to a farmer after he has paid all costs (excluding water charges) and an allowance is made for family living. Predictions about variations in payment capacity are extemely useful from the planning stance; for example larger farm units might be allocated to land with a lower payment capacity. To achieve such an assessment, information has to be collected not only about physical attributes, but also data necessary to predict crop yields. The scheme is a specialised form of a land

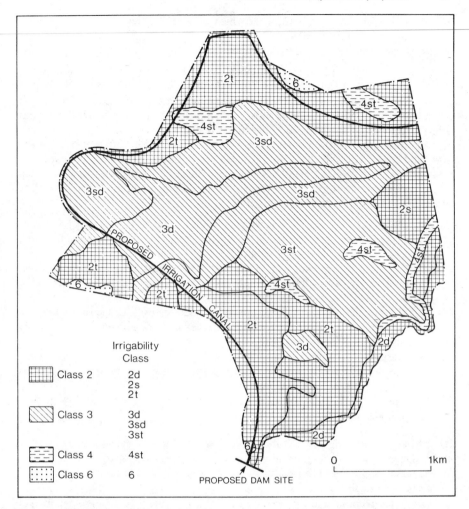

Fig. 4.1 The Chalimbana area of Zambia according to suitability for irrigation (classes are described in the text) (From Yager, Lee and Perfect, 1967).

classification survey and a standardised method for recording and presenting information through the use of symbols is integral to the method. The scheme does not specify critical factors in order to define the land classes since projects vary in area, development goals and economic circumstances. As such the USBR scheme is best described as a framework. However, all projects using the scheme categorise land into the following classes albeit on different bases:

Class 1. Highest level of irrigation suitability and highest payment capacity.
Class 2. Intermediate suitability and payment capacity.
Class 3. Lowest suitability and payment capacity.
Class 4. A special use class such as 4F (fruit), or this class indicates land with excessive deficiencies which have been shown to be irrigable through economic and engineering studies.

Class 5. A special class indicating land which requires further investigation before classification is possible.

Class 6. Unsuitable for irrigation development.

Maletic and Hutchings (1967) include tables from studies dealing with parts of South Dakota and Hawaii to illustrate how the definitions of three classes (1 to 3) vary according to particular projects. The Zambian study by Yager, Lee and Perfect (1967) also adopted the USBR classification scheme. Subclasses are represented by various letters as previously mentioned to indicate particular deficiencies.

As already stated, the USBR scheme has been applied in different parts of the world and has provided the basis for the development of schemes tailored to particular areas. For example, New Zealand has a land classification scheme for irrigation based on the American one (Griffiths, 1975). In the New Zealand method, five irrigability classes are defined and can be summarised as follows:

Class 1. Highly suitable for irrigation with negligible obstacles. Topography is flat, soils are well drained, of moderate permeability, and are deep, medium textured, with good available water capacity.

Class 2. Suitable for irrigation with slight obstacles such as undulating topography, moderately well drained soils, moderately slow or moderately rapid permeability or moderate depth of soil.

Class 3. Moderately suitable for irrigation with moderate obstacles such as easy rolling topography, imperfect or somewhat excessively drained soils, slow or rapid permeability, or shallow soils.

Class 4. Marginally suitable for irrigation with severe obstacles, such as rolling topography, poorly or excessively drained soils, very slow or very rapid permeability or very shallow soils.

Class 5. Unsuitable for normal irrigation with very severe obstacles in topography, drainage or soils.

(From Griffiths, 1975, p. 14)

It can be appreciated immediately that these classes are defined according to soil, relief and drainage characteristics. The monograph by Griffiths (1975) specifies in detail how individual characteristics are observed or measured and a table defines in detail the nature of the irrigability classes.

Examples of completed projects designed to investigate the irrigation potential of particular areas can be selected from studies by the Land Resources division of the Ministry of Overseas Development (UK). Work has been done in Ethiopia (Makin *et al.*, 1976) and in Botswana (Mitchell, 1976). A short paragraph in this book can do little justice to these impressive investigations. The Ethiopian survey around Lake Zwai is comprehensive, covering such topics as the evaluation of the water resources and agricultural potential which leads to proposals for irrigation development and subsequent economic analysis. The land classification is based on the USBR scheme and the results indicate that the overall area suitable for irrigation is restricted more by soil and topography than by availability of water. The study in eastern Botswana by Mitchell (1976) is more limited in objective since his prime concern was to assess the irrigation potential of soils. The survey is a reconnaissance one with maps at a scale of 1 : 500 000 showing irrigation potential. Land facets are the basic mapping units which are evaluated in terms of irrigation potential using the method of Thomas and Thompson (1959), but modified to meet local needs and which also conform broadly with the land classes of the USBR scheme. Land facets were delimited by the analysis of patterns on aerial photographs. Such patterns resulted from variations in landform (relief, degree of dissection, steepness and shape of slope) and lithological differences. Thus the identified land facets were areas of land with similar drainage density and slope characteristics, with similar lithology and consequently similar soils. In essence the land system approach was adopted (section 3.6). Field surveys were then necessary to describe and sample soil types in the various facets and such information allowed the estimation of irrigation potential.

The techniques discussed in this section so far have been concerned with soil or land classification schemes designed to define irrigability classes. Parametric methods in the sense defined in section 3.5 have also been used. The aim of these methods is the production of some index to express such suitability. Bowser and Moss (1950) trace the development of soil rating methods relevant to irrigation, and they describe how the Saskatchewan Soil Survey in 1936 began to carry out such research although similar work had been initiated in Alberta by 1930. Bowser and Moss propose that the rating of soils for irrigation should follow the same basic approach as the rating of soils for unirrigated agriculture though, of course, different emphasis has to be given to soil characteristics. For example, in a semi-arid area, a top rating might be given to a heavy textured soil for unirrigated agriculture whilst for irrigation purposes, prime significance would be given to soils of medium texture. Bowser and Moss propose that the following seven factors ought to be considered in classifying and rating soils for irrigation: soil profile type, nature of soil parent material, soil texture, salinity, degree of stoniness, erosion hazard and topography. These seven factors are subdivided into component type. The resultant seven ratings are multiplied together to give an overall score which allows the classification of a site according to its suitability for irrigation. Bowser and Moss thus produced a well-defined parametric method for rating soils though they stressed that it was to be used only as a fairly specific guide since personal judgement was still required to check on the results. They also appreciated that irrigation may well change key soil properties and thus account must be taken of this in the evaluation procedure.

The study by Bowser and Moss was rather advanced for its day since it is only in more recent years that parametric methods of soil assessment have become common (section 3.5). It is instructive to consider the parametric method proposed by Sys and Verheye (1974) since there are clear similarities with the Bowser and Moss (1950) approach. Sys and Verheye (1974) state that the suitability of soils for irrigation in arid and semi-arid areas is mainly influenced by seven factors, viz. texture, soil depth, calcium carbonate content, gypsum status, salinity and alkalinity content, soil drainage and slope. The value of an overall index is obtained by multiplying ratings which are listed in tables by Sys and Verheye. It is then possible to assign sites to one of five classes ranging from very suitable to completely unsuitable. The Sys and Verheye method gives greater emphasis to soil chemical properties than is the case with the Bowser and Moss (1950) rating index.

As was stressed at the beginning of this section, the assessment of soils is only one component of the planning process for irrigation schemes. The appropriate techniques of soil investigation depend on the stage and scale of the project. Introductory reconnaissance level studies of the type carried out by Mitchell (1976) in Botswana must be followed by intensive investigations in the proposed areas of irrigation. At this detailed level, increasing emphasis must be placed upon field experiments to measure such values as hydraulic conductivity or infiltration rate followed by the laboratory analysis of soils. Guidance on appropriate laboratory methods is given by Loveday Beatty and Norris (1972) and Loveday (1974).

4.3 SOIL INTERPRETATION FOR URBAN DEVELOPMENT

As stressed in Chapter 1, soils of particular agricultural value ought to be retained wherever possible for that use and not transferred to non-agricultural purposes. Thus in terms of soil interpretation for urban development, the results should indicate where such development ought not to take place. Soil survey data are also of value for the planning of urban areas. Such information can be used to predict a range of problems which can be encountered in the construction of new houses and provision of associated services. Unfavourable soil conditions can cause problems in terms of structural stability of buildings, corrosion of concrete pipes, failure of septic tanks, pollution from rubbish being buried in unsuitable soils, or cracking and pot-holing of roads laid on poorly suited soils. The results of soil surveys in proposed new urban areas can be of great assistance in identifying special design precautions which will be necessary to deal with specific soil problems. The cost benefit of such surveys in the USA has been estimated by Klingebiel (1966) as 1 to 100. A similar cost–benefit ratio has been obtained for Massachusetts where Zayach (1973) has calculated that there is more than a $110 benefit for each dollar invested in a soil survey. Given the very clear cost advantages, it is perhaps surprising that soil surveys geared to urban needs have not become very common, though there are a few clear exceptions. In Britain, the tradition is for urban areas to be excluded from routine soil survey.

Credit must be given to the Americans for first encouraging the application of soil survey data to urban needs. Pettry and Coleman (1973) describe how Fairfax County in Virginia was the first to employ a soil scientist for multipurpose soil interpretation on a county basis and had an urban soil programme in operation by 1955. Support for such a programme resulted from mistakes being made in selecting sites for schools and other buildings where extra costs were incurred through ignorance of soil conditions. Widespread publicity of these avoidable costly ventures clearly indicated the need for an urban soil programme. Failure of septic tank systems also caused much alarm; some of these tanks had been installed in soils with seasonally high water tables. The urban soil survey was able to locate areas with seasonally high water tables and soils which were too shallow, as well as areas subject to periodic flooding. Pettry and Coleman (1973) also describe problems of structural stability to illustrate the value of urban soil survey in Fairfax County. Unusually deep snow occurred during the winter of 1961, and landslides followed the ultimate thaw. It was discovered that these slides occurred on soils of similar type, namely where marine clays were overlain by sandy soils. Such soils have now been mapped and building permits are only issued if a method of minimising slide susceptibility has been designed. Soils which expand in volume according to moisture content (certain clays, for example montmorillonite), also pose problems for the construction and maintenance of roads.

The writings of Lindo Bartelli have for long been geared to publicising the application of soil survey data in America. In 1962 he argued that contractors, farmers, area planners, engineers and home owners ought to have the basic results of a soil survey and in a form appropriate to their needs. He demonstrates how detailed soil maps can be used to predict certain constructional difficulties. Tabled 4.1 shows which engineering properties can be deduced from soil characteristics. The table also indicates how soil surveys can aid with locating fill material for foundations of buildings or roads. Of course, such interpretation from soil maps does not mean that more detailed site investigations and laboratory analyses will not be necessary; however, as Bartelli (1962) stresses, the interpretation of soil maps allows the recognition of troublesome soils at an earlier stage. The book by Bartelli *et al.* (1966) includes several papers which indicate

Table 4.1   List of engineering properties of soils which can be deduced from soil properties and characteristics (From Bartelli, 1962, p. 101).

SOIL CHARACTERISTICS AND PROPERTIES	ENGINEERING PROPERTIES
Undisturbed soil	
Texture, pH drainage	Metal conduit corrosion potential
Drainage, texture, kind of clay, organic matter content	Suitability for road subgrades
Drainage, texture, kind of clay, organic matter content	Suitability for building foundations
Drainage, texture	Susceptibility to frost action
Texture, kind of clay, organic matter content	Shrink–swell potential
Texture and structure of B and C horizons	Percolation rate
Surface texture, permeability, drainage	Trafficability (non-vehicular)
Disturbed soil	
Texture, kind of clay, organic matter content	Suitability as fill material
Texture, organic matter content	Suitability as lining for water storage units
Texture, organic matter content	Suitability as topsoil

the application of soil surveys to urban planning in the USA during the early 1960s.

The application of soil information is best illustrated by discussion of an example and a study by Murtha and Reid (1976) of the Townsville area in Queensland, Australia, is selected. Townsville is situated at the mouth of the Ross river (Fig. 4.2). To the north and west of this river a featureless plain, broken only by a few inselbergs, gradually rises to piedmont slopes which fringe the base of a coastal scarp. The land to the south of the Ross river is dominated by various mountain ranges with limited areas of alluvium along the major streams. A littoral zone composed of mangroves, mudflats, salt pan and beach ridges is extensive.

The soil maps accompanying the report are at a scale of 1 : 100 000 and an extract at a reduced scale is given in Fig. 4.2. Eight broad soil groups are present; groups 6, 7 and 8 also form mapping units whilst groups 1 to 5 are subdivided into more detailed units. The soils of the eight broad classes can be summarised as follows:

1. Cracking clays

These soils expand and contract according to moisture content. The grey clays (1a) occur chiefly on the main plains and on the backswamp deposits of the larger alluvial plains and are distinguished by the presence of gilgai microrelief. The black earths (1b) occur on alluvium of more local origin, on floodplains of smaller streams and on gentle piedmont slopes of areas of basic parent material. Gilgai microrelief is only weakly developed. Mapping unit 1c is also a grey clay, but areas mapped in this category are subject to prolonged flooding.

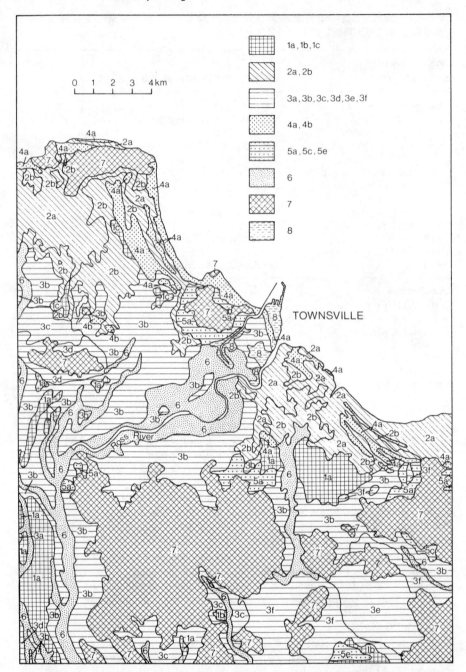

Fig. 4.2   Soils in the Townsville area, Australia. The legend is provided in Table 4.2 (From Murtha and Reid, 1976).

Table 4.2 Description of soils present in Fig. 4.2 (From Murtha and Reid, 1976).

DOMINANT SOIL		MAJOR CHARACTERISTICS OF DOMINANT SOIL	URBAN DEVELOPMENT LIMITATIONS		
Map unit	GSG *		Agronomic	Engineering	Landscaping
1a	Grey clay	Gilgaied cracking clays with dark grey, strong medium blocky-structured heavy clay A horizons over grey or grey-brown, coarse blocky heavy clay subsoils. May be mottled at depth.	Severe. Low fertility, slow internal drainage, poor surface drainage (water ponded in depressions).	Expansive clays cause problems in all engineering applications. Surface drainage very slow.	Severe limitations, difficult plant establishment, few adapted species, limited access due to water ponding.
1b	Black	Very dark grey to black, strong fine blocky-structured heavy clay A horizons over dark grey or black coarse blocky heavy clay subsoils. Moderate to high amounts of carbonate below 30 cm. May become grey or brown at depth.	Moderately severe. Low to moderate fertility, slow internal drainage. Poor surface drainage where there are gilgai.	As above.	As above.
1c	Grey clay	Dark grey heavy clay A horizons with prominent gley mottles. Subsoils are dark grey heavy clays with prominent olive-grey, orange and red mottles.	Severe. Flooded for prolonged periods each year. Some flooding by tidal waters.	Expansive clays, flooding, shallow water table.	As above, some flooding by saline waters.
2a	Solonchak	Dark brown saline muds under mangroves and saline clays on salt pan.	Very severe. Subject to tidal inundation, very high salt levels.	Subject to tidal inundation and storm surge. Low bearing strength for foundations.	Limited to salt-tolerant species.
2b	Solodic	Thin (10–15 cm) strongly bleached silty loam or clay loam A horizons over dark grey or dark grey-brown heavy clays, strongly mottled yellow and red at depth.	Very severe. High salt levels due to occasional tidal inundation, low fertility.	Subject to tidal flooding. Permanent water table at about 60 cm.	As above.
3a	Solodised solonetz	Very thin (15 cm) strongly bleached silty or sandy loam A horizons with abrupt change to brownish or greyish heavy clay B horizons. Alkaline reaction in subsoils.	Very severe. Moderate to high salt and very high exchangeable sodium in the clay B horizon. Very poor physical properties, low fertility, impeded drainage.	B horizon clays have very poor drainage and low bearing capacity when wet. They are highly dispersive with adverse chemical properties causing corrosion of underground services.	Very severe limitations, few adapted species, soil amelioration difficult and costly.

Table 4.2 (continued)

Map unit	GSG	MAJOR CHARACTERISTICS OF DOMINANT SOIL	URBAN DEVELOPMENT LIMITATIONS		
			Agronomic	Engineering	Landscaping
3b	Solodic, solodised solonetz	Very thin (2–5 cm), light grey-brown sandy or silty loam A₁ over very strongly bleached sandy loam A₂. Total A horizon depth ranges from 15 to 25 cm. Abrupt change to whole coloured or mottled grey or yellowish heavy clay B horizons with alkaline reaction.	Severe. Similar to 3a, but as depth of A horizon increases severity of limitation lessens.	As for 3a but as depth of A horizon increases, engineering properties improve. May be some expansive clays in the B horizon and many are highly dispersive.	Severe limitations, impeded drainage, limited species adaptability. Need to import loam for lawn establishment.
3c	Solodic	As above but total A horizon depth exceeds 25 cm, may be as deep as 80 cm.	Moderate, as for 3b.	As for 3b.	As above but limitations are less severe.
3d	Solodic	Thin (3–5 cm), light grey-brown sandy or silty loam A₁ horizon over very strongly bleached sandy loam A₂ horizon. Abrupt change to mottled light grey or yellow-grey heavy clay B horizons with mildly to strongly acid reaction.	Moderate, as for 3b, but internal drainage is better.	As for 3b, but limitations less severe.	As for 3c.
3e	Red podzolic	Dark brown or dark grey-brown loam A₁ and slightly paler loam A₂ horizon. Abrupt change at 10–15 cm to dark red, strong blocky-structured medium clay B horizon grading to weathered parent material from 60 cm.	No major limitations, reasonable nutrient levels and fair internal drainage.	Nil.	Few limitations. Many adapted species available.
3f	Yellow and brown podzolic	Dark grey-brown sandy loam to loam A₁ over weakly developed A₂ horizon. Abrupt change at 15–25 cm to yellow or brown, medium to heavy clay, blocky-structured B horizons.	No major limitations. Moderate fertility levels, internal drainage may be slow but not excessively impeded.	May encounter some of the problems associated with units 3a and 3b, but much less severe.	As above.
4a	Siliceous sand	Uniform coarse sands. Profile development dependent on age of beach ridge.	Severe. Extremely low fertility, very low water-holding capacity.	Subject to erosion and storm surge on beach fronts, may require compaction and stabilisation for foundations.	Limited by low water availability. No restriction with supplementary irrigation and fertilization.

Table 4.2 (continued)

DOMINANT SOIL		MAJOR CHARACTERISTICS OF DOMINANT SOIL	URBAN DEVELOPMENT LIMITATIONS		
Map unit	GSG		Agronomic	Engineering	Landscaping
4b	Siliceous sand	Uniform sands with deep, very strongly bleached A_2 horizon and mottled pale yellow, colour B horizon.	Severe. Very low fertility, low water-holding capacity.	May require compaction and stabilisation for foundations.	As above.
5a	Red earth	Grey-brown loamy sand to sandy loam A horizons overlying red or yellowish red sandy clay loam to sandy clay B horizons.	Moderate fertility levels, no major limitations.	No restrictions.	Very few restrictions, large range of adapted species.
5c	Yellow earth	Grey-brown loamy sand or sandy loam A horizons overlying yellow or reddish yellow sandy clay loam B horizons which grade to coarse gravels below 1–1.5 m.	Moderate to low fertility, no other restrictions.	No restrictions.	Few restrictions, large range of adapted species, fertilisation advisable.
5e	Yellow earth	Dark grey-brown loam A_1 horizons overlying mottled yellow-brown and red clay loam to light clay B horizons. Abrupt change to heavy clay D horizons at about 60–80 cm.	Moderate to low fertility, impeded drainage at 60–80 cm.	Sink hole and gilgai microrelief, expansive clay D horizons cause problems with road and building foundations.	As for unit 3c.
6	Alluvial soil, red earth	Wide range of soils on younger alluvium.	No restrictions other than likelihood of flooding.	Subject to flooding, otherwise no restrictions.	No restriction of species, use may be restricted due to flooding.
7		Very wide range of soils on hilly and mountainous terrain. All soils have gravel on surface and throughout the profile. Rock outcrop is common.	Similar soils would be expected to behave as in the groups already described.	Instability of steep slopes a major problem. Difficult to provide access and services in many areas.	
8		Reclaimed land. Including dumping of domestic and industrial wastes and sand pumping.		Subsidence of fill material and in many areas the low bearing strength of underlying mangrove mud is a major restriction.	Little restriction although adequate top dressing needed for lawn establishment.

Degree of severity followed by major limiting factors. In soils with marked texture contrast unified classification of both surface soil and subsoil is given.

*GSG Great Soil Group.

2. Saline soils

The salinity of these soils is due to flooding by tidal waters. Soils of the solonchak mapping unit (2a) correspond to areas of mangroves and saline clays on salt pans. Map unit 2b has a solodic soil as the dominant type; this soil is subject to occasional tidal inundation and is further distinguished by a strongly bleached A horizon overlying dark mottled clays.

3. Duplex soils

This group encompasses a range of soils, but their common characteristic is the contrast in texture between the upper and lower horizons. Map units 3a, 3b, 3c and 3d are dominated by solodic and solodised solonetz soils. These soils are distinguished by a thin, light grey-brown sandy loam A_1 horizon overlying a very strongly bleached A_2 horizon of the same texture. In marked contrast the B horizon has a clay texture. Solodic and solonetz soils both have saline C horizons and the former has a distinctive blocky structure in the B horizon compared with a strong columnar one for the latter. A solodised solonetz soil has a strongly bleached A_2 horizon which is not present in a solonetz. The detailed differences between map units 3a, 3b, 3c and 3d can be appreciated by study of Table 4.2 which accompanies Fig. 4.2. The other duplex soils are the red podzolics for map unit 3e and the yellow and brown podzolics for map unit 3f. These soils are all acidic and have a contrast in texture from loams or sandy loams in the upper horizons to clays in the B horizons. They all have weakly developed bleached A_2 horizons and are subdivided according to the colour of the B horizons.

4. Uniform sands

These soils occur on the beach ridges fringing the coastline and on older stranded beach ridges. Soils in map unit 4a are formed on coarse siliceous sand and the degree of profile development depends upon the age of the beach ridges. With soils in map unit 4b, also formed on siliceous sand, a bleached A_2 horizon is very evident as well as a mottled B horizon. These soils occur on the older beach ridges.

5. Gradational soils

The duplex soils exhibit a sharp contrast in texture within their profiles whilst gradational soils vary more gradually in texture. In the map extract only map units 5a (red earth) and 5c and 5e (yellow earths) are represented. A red earth with an unbleached A_2 horizon present, has an acid reaction throughout the profile. The texture grades from loamy sand or sandy loam in the A_1 horizon, to sandy clay loam or light sandy clay in the B horizon. Red earth soils occur on piedmont slopes. The yellow earth soils are more variable than the red earths, though they have similar general profiles. Fairly obviously the B horizons of the red earths are dominantly red compared with yellow for the yellow earths.

6. Soils on young alluvium

This soil group is included in one map unit (6) and embraces a wide range of soils developed on young alluvial floodplains, terraces and levees. The most extensive areas of soils mapped in this unit flank the lower course of the Ross river.

7. Soils on hilly and mountainous terrain

This map unit includes a very wide range of soils, though they all have gravel on their surfaces and throughout their profiles. Extensive areas of map unit 7 occur to the immediate south of Townsville (Mount Suart Range) and to the south-east (Muntalunga Range).

8. Reclaimed land

Soils in this unit are man-made through the dumping of domestic and industrial wastes and sand pumping. They occur within and adjacent to the urban area of Townsville.

The major characteristics of the dominant soil in each map unit are summarised in Table 4.2 which accompanies Fig. 4.2. The table also gives a summary of agronomic, engineering and landscaping limitations posed by soil conditions, information which Murtha and Reid (1976) consider useful for the planning of urban development. These three groups of limitations merit consideration in turn.

In an assessment of soils for urban planning, information on soil suitability for agriculture is usually included so that new urban areas are not zoned on the better land. This is not the case for the Townsville area since the surrounding region is low-density beef cattle grazing land. Thus Murtha and Reid (1976) recommend that urban development should take place on soils with lesser agronomic limitations since these soils generally have fewer engineering limitations. In detail they suggest that the better types of soil should be reserved for public facilities or open space with urban development planned around these more favoured soils, though some soils pose so many difficulties that they should not be used for any purpose.

Table 4.2 also illustrates how information relevant to engineering can be presented according to soil map unit. Structural failures and foundation failures of roads occur in Townsville because of a lack of understanding of soil physical and chemical properties (Murtha and Reid, 1976). Particular problems are posed by the expansive clays (map unit 1) which also occur in the duplex soils (map unit 3). Soils with moderate to high levels of exchangeable sodium in their subsoils are highly susceptible to gully erosion. This implies that great care must be taken in the design of drains. Road failures can often be linked with the use of highly dispersive clays as foundation materials. Galvanised steel pipes corrode very rapidly if laid in the B horizons of the duplex soils which are highly alkaline, and have moderate to high exchangeable sodium and moderate salt levels. Some subsoils of the cracking clays and duplex groups also have significant sulphate contents which would indicate a concrete corrosion problem. Again, remedial measures are necessary.

The final column in Table 4.2 shows how soil information can be interpreted to aid the landscaping of the Townsville area where the tasks are to stabilise the foreshore, plant trees along streets, improve school yards and playgrounds, plant parks and develop urban gardens. The foreshore problem is essentially one of trying to stabilise the movement of sand by establishing sand-binding plants. Along the highways and streets, the need is to select trees, shrubs or plants appropriate to soil conditions. For example, the duplex soils pose severe limitations to tree growth. Soils which are poorly drained and which puddle under heavy pedestrian usage when wet, are unsuitable for school yards and playgrounds unless expensive treatment is undertaken. Murtha and Reid (1976) also argue that the home gardener can save much money and effort if he knows the potential or limitations of the soil type on which he is situated in relation to plant species.

This Queensland study well demonstrates how soil map units can be interpreted to aid land use planning within urban areas. The project was concerned with mapping 212 000 ha and the published map is at a scale of 1 : 100 000. For detailed planning a more intensive survey is necessary, exemplified in Australia by an urban capability study for an area of 445 ha near Banora Point in New South Wales (Manson and Greaves, 1977). The soils of this area were mapped at a scale of 1 : 4 000 and then samples were analysed in the laboratory with an emphasis on physical properties. The following properties were determined: sand, silt and clay contents, coherence of soil aggregates, shrink–swell potential, liquid limit, plastic limit, the soil type according to the Unified Soil Classification System, the dispersal index and the erodibility index. These terms are described in appendix 1. An urban land capability scheme is presented with five major land classes of erosion/instability hazard, viz:

CLASS	EROSION/INSTABILITY HAZARD	URBAN CAPABILITY
A	Low	Extensive building complexes, industrial, commercial, residential
B	Moderate	Industrial, commercial, residential
C	High	Residential
D	Very high	Reserves and open space for recreation
E	Extreme	Not recommended for development

These five classes are subdivided into subclasses according to the major physical constraints to development potential. These are:

1. Slope.
2. Flooding.
3. Soil characteristic.
4. Extraction/disposal site.
5. Topographic feature (swamp, seepage).
6. High water table.

An example is B-3, defined as posing a moderate hazard with there being a swelling soil constraint. Such land is suitable for residential development. The same approach is also adopted by Junor, Emery and Crouch (1977) in a *Land resources study of the Albury–Wodonga growth centre in New South Wales.*

A study of soils to aid the planning of the Christchurch region in New Zealand is interesting because the scheme for classifying soils according to their suitability for urban uses includes an assessment of agricultural value (Raeside and Rennie, 1974). Soils are mapped at the series and phase level and phases are assigned to the following classes and subclasses:

Class A   Soils suitable for all kinds of urban uses.

   Subclass A1   Soils suitable for all kinds of urban use, but not of high actual or potential value for food production.

   Subclass A2   Soils suitable for all kinds of urban use and also of high actual and potential value for food production.

Class B   Soils suitable for restricted kinds of urban use.

   Subclass B1   Soils of flat to undulating land unsuitable for residential use, for example peat soils.

Subclass B2   Soils of rolling and hilly land, unsuitable for commercial and industrial uses.

Class C   Soils unsuitable for urban use without substantial modification.

Subclass C1   Soils of flat to rolling land, for example limitations of high water tables requiring regional drainage; liability to flood and requiring flood control.

Subclass C2   Soils of hilly and steep land, for example limitations of erosion, slope and difficult access.

(From Raeside and Rennie, 1974, pp. 62–3.)

In addition, information is given in a table about each soil phase according to land uses for which it is best suited, its value for food production and recommended land use zoning. Clearly, such a report provides an excellent starting point in the evolution of a land use development plan.

In Canada there is also much interest in the application of soil survey data to urban planning. For example the soil survey of Halton County in Ontario (Gillespie, Wicklund and Miller, n.d.) provides not only a soil capability assessment for agriculture but also suitability ratings of individual soil series for urban and suburban use. In a table, ratings are given in terms of suitablility for septic tank operation, home site location, roads, underground utilities and as a source of gravel. The information is designed to provide some general guidelines at the preliminary planning stage, and must be followed by more detailed site investigation before construction is started. A similar approach is adopted in the survey of Waterloo County in Ontario (Presant and Wicklund, 1971), though in this study greater emphasis is given to the engineering properties of the soils. This is possible through the laboratory determination of a range of physical attributes of soils similar to the Banora Point investigation in Australia (Manson and Greaves, 1977). Such information combined with the standard soil survey data allowed the soils in Waterloo County to be arranged into seven engineering soil groups. Thus each soil series is assigned to an engineering group. Comments are also made about the soil characteristics of each series affecting highway and road construction, shallow excavations and septic tank installations.

For a Canadian example of a soil survey geared specifically to urban planning needs, mention must be made of the study by Lindsay, Scheelar and Twardy (1973). In this case, a soil survey programme was integral to the planning process for Mill Woods, a new suburb of Edmonton in Alberta. Soils were examined on a grid pattern with the distance between grid intersections being 76.2 m. Soil samples were collected at every second intersection and analysed for water-soluble salts, electrical conductivity, soil reaction (pH), particle size distribution, Atterberg limits and total nitrogen and total carbon contents. Soils were then evaluated in terms of landscaping potential. Some, for example, had fairly serious limitations with regard to establishing lawns. The solonetzic soils which were mapped posed problems with respect to compaction and trafficability. A major engineering hazard which emerged from the survey was the potential corrosion of concrete structures and underground conduits because of subsoil salinity in certain soils.

Similar types of studies could be described from the USA to illustrate how soils are assessed for urban planning. Bauer (1973), in a general review, presents suitability ratings of soils in south-east Wisconsin for rural and urban land use planning. The continuing and increasing need for the application of soil data to urban and suburban development in the USA is stressed by McCormack and Bartelli (1977). For a specific example, reference can be made to the study by Zaporozec and Hole (1976). They provide suitability maps for urban development, absorption of septic tank effluent, field crops, erodibility and livestock for Langlade County in north-central Wisconsin. They then discuss the various planning strategies posed by these maps in terms of the urban expansion from the settlement of Antigo. At a more detailed level they illustrate how soil as well as geological and locational information can assist with the choice of new sites for the disposal of solid waste near the city of Madison in Wisconsin.

No reference has been made so far to the use of soil information in British urban planning. This is not because no work has been done on this topic, but because few reports are available. The Soil Surveys of England and Wales and of Scotland do provide information to planning authorities as a result of specific requests, but guidance is probably most sought on the agricultural value of soils. However, Hartnup (1976) mentions that soil maps influenced the planning decisions in the location of Skelmersdale new town (Lancashire) where development was steered on to the least valuable agricultural land. Little work has been done in Britain in terms of assessing soils specifically for urban needs similar to the studies quoted in Australia, New Zealand, Canada and the USA. One exception is the special soil survey carried out by Hartnup and Jarvis (1973) who assessed the soils in the Castleford area of Yorkshire in terms of capability for agricultural, recreational and urban uses. The area of 34 km² was mapped at the series level, though three series were subdivided into phases. Soil samples were analysed for selected engineering properties, for example, liquid limit, plastic limit, dry density, apparent angle of shearing resistance, coefficient of volume change, coefficient of consolidation and grading, as well as for the more routine attributes of agricultural relevance. The results of importance to planners are presented in the form of tables from which information on attributes of soils which affect various land uses may be extracted. One example is a table giving the suitabilities of different soil mapping units for buildings, road construction and services. Mention should also be made of research done in Britain on the use of soil information for roadworks (McGown and Iley, 1973) and on the relationship between soil map units and soil corrosiveness (Corcoran et al., 1977).

In general terms, therefore, soil assessment for urban needs has followed a similar pattern to that for agriculture. Broad schemes of assessment for urban requirements are used, for example the New Zealand study of Raeside and Rennie (1974), but soils are normally evaluated for specific uses such as residential development, and commercial and industrial development. Soils are also interpreted to predict engineering limitations. Such applications are not limited to urban areas but are also used in rural areas. In North America septic tanks are widely used in rural areas for disposing of liquid household wastes and soil surveys can very much aid the selection of appropriate sites (Beatty and Bouma, 1973). Coen and Holland (1976) have carried out a soil survey of Waterton Lakes National Park in Alberta, Canada, with the aim of identifying some of the soil attributes relevant to specific recreational uses. These will be discussed in the next section (4.4), but the Albertan study also assesses soils for septic tank installations, permanent buildings and local roads. Obviously the techniques applied in this very rural locality can also assist in the planning of urban areas.

It should be pointed out that there are other types of surveys which are helpful to urban planning. Geomorphological mapping has proved useful to highway engineering design (Brunsden et al., 1975) and no doubt could also be developed for urban planning. Geological surveys are also appropriate; for example, Cratchley and Denness (1972) describe how a detailed survey assisted in the planning of the new town of Milton Keynes, Buckinghamshire, England, though they state that the geological work ought to have been carried out at an earlier stage to have given maximum planning benefits.

Stratigraphical units were regrouped into engineering geology units in a similar way to the regrouping of soils in the Waterloo study (Presant and Wicklund, 1971). Information was thus made available for predicting a range of problems likely to be encountered in constructional activities.

The examples described earlier in this section lend clear support to the view of Bauer (who is a planner) that 'a detailed operational soil survey, therefore, is one of the soundest investments of public funds that can be made' (Bauer, 1973, p. 25). However, some concluding cautionary comments should be made regarding the application of soil information to urban planning. Soil maps, regardless of scale, always show mapping units which possess a certain degree of internal variability. Thus, even within areas designated suitable for houses, there may well be localised soil conditions which do not permit such construction without substantial extra costs being incurred. For planning purposes, detailed site investigation must therefore follow from the initial assessment. Basic problems associated with classification can also arise if soils defined according to pedological or agronomic criteria have to be classed according to some aspect of urban development. For example, a certain amount of variation in clay content might be acceptable in a soil series defined according to pedological criteria, but such variation could be unacceptable within one mapping unit for constructional purposes. Ideally soil surveys ought to be designed from the beginning for fairly specific purposes and this is now being done for many urban areas, especially in the USA. The cost benefits of such research are clearly evident and there is every indication that planning authorities concerned with urban areas will increasingly realise the merits of urban soil surveys.

4.4 SOIL ASSESSMENT FOR RECREATION

To conclude this chapter, consideration is given to the use of soil surveys in planning for recreation. As pressures continue to grow on the land, every effort must be made to ensure that land uses and land use activities are carefully matched with the nature of the soil. This is particularly true for recreation where the pressures are becoming increasingly evident (Simmons, 1974). There is a need in the planning and management of recreational areas for relevant information about soil conditions.

Recreation encompasses a wide range of land uses and land use activities from wilderness areas where every effort is made to prevent man from intruding upon the landscape to intensively used country parks or picnic areas. Given the diversity of uses and activities which can occur under the label 'recreation', it is usual for soil conditions to be assessed with respect to particular uses or activities. However, there are comprehensive schemes for assessing suitability for overall recreational use. In Chapter 2, the land capability classification for recreation by the Canada Land Inventory was described; this scheme defines seven classes of land which are differentiated on the basis of the intensity of outdoor recreation which can be generated and sustained. This land capability approach to recreation is much broader than an assessment of soils in terms of recreation. The Canadian method incorporates a judgement on landscape attraction and indeed there is also a range of techniques which have been used for assessing scenic quality, reviewed by the Countryside Commission for Scotland (1971). For present purposes, consideration is limited to specific soil properties of importance to recreation.

All soils can be used for some form of recreation, but equally some soils can pose particular problems, a theme discussed by Montgomery and Edminster (1966). Clearly, soils which are poorly drained provide difficulties for campsites, roads, trails, playgrounds and picnic areas. Some soils may only be subject to high water tables at

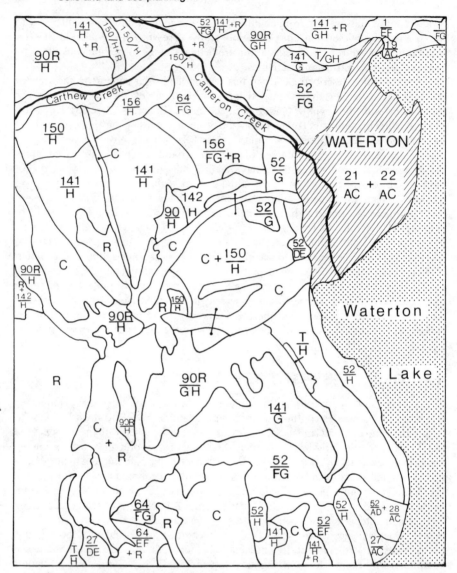

Fig. 4.3 Soils in part of Waterton Lakes National Park, Alberta, Canada. The legend is provided in Table 4.3 (From Coen and Holland, 1976). Scale *c.* 1:24 000.

particular times of the year and may be quite satisfactory for these purposes at other times. The ability of soil to withstand the trampling of feet is very important. Soils with a high clay content become sticky when wet and may well become puddled. Such structural damage then impairs the growth of grass, and in the extreme, bare patches may develop. Stony or shallow soils create difficulties for constructing flat playgrounds or campsites. Campsites, or picnic areas have to provide toilet facilities, and often it is not possible to connect these with the sewerage system. Instead, dependence has to be placed upon septic tanks and again soil conditions are important in aiding the selection of appropriate sites.

Table 4.3   Legend to Fig. 4.3. (Extracted from Table 2 in Coen and Holland, 1976, pp. 37–8).

SOIL MAP UNIT	SUBGROUP CLASSIFICATION	LANDFORMS
1	Orthic dark brown and orthic black chernozemic soils	Glaciofluvial terraces, eskers, kames, outwash plains
19	Rego black and orthic black chernozemic soils	Alluvial terraces, floodplains
21	Orthic regosol	
22	Orthic dark brown chernozemic soils	
27	Cumulic and orthic regosols	Alluvial fans
32	Orthic humic gleysol	
52	Orthic eutric brunisols	
64	Orthic humo-ferric podzol	Moraines
141	Orthic regosol	
142	Orthic regosol	
150	Orthic regosols and eluviated eutric brunisols	Upper mountain sides (steep land)
156	Orthic humo-ferric podzols and eluviated eutric brunisols	
90R	Orthic regosols, lithic phase	
R	Not soil; rock outcrops, mountain tops, solid and broken rock	Miscellaneous landforms, complexes
T	Not soil; talus (broken rock fragments plus fines)	
C	Chutes (mainly regosolic soils)	

Topographic classes

Class	Slope (%)
A	0.0–0.5
B	0.5–2
C	2–5
D	5–9
E	9–15
F	15–30
G	30–60
H	over 60

Map symbol convention

The number in the map symbol identifies the map unit and hence the kinds of soils within it. The letter beneath the number identifies the slope classes associated with the map unit. For example, the symbol $\frac{21}{AD}$ identifies orthic regosols having A to D slopes.

As in the previous two sections of this chapter, an example is selected to illustrate the assessment techniques for a particular locality. The chosen study is the one already mentioned by Coen and Holland (1976) dealing with the Waterton Lakes National Park, Alberta, Canada. The area is located in the extreme south of the state and adjoins Glacier National Park in Montana. The soil survey was part of a resource inventory initiated by the National Parks Service. The park, about 526 km² in extent, lies dominantly within the Rocky Mountains and has a landscape varying from plainland to deeply incised valleys and to rugged mountain peaks. Such diversity of relief clearly presented major difficulties to the field survey of soils and much reliance had to be placed upon the interpretation of aerial photographs. Emphasis was given to delimiting landforms (for example, glaciofluvial terraces, eskers, kames, river terraces, floodplains, alluvial fans, moraines, etc.) which were further subdivided according to soil morphological features such as mottles indicative of poor drainage conditions, texture and stoniness. Field survey allowed boundaries to be checked and representative soil profiles were described and sampled from each map unit. A total of fifty-eight map units plus a number of miscellaneous land areas (for example snowchutes, and areas of rock outcrops) were described and mapped. An extract from the resultant maps is shown in Fig. 4.3. As can be seen from this figure and the associated legend (Table 4.3), information is given for each mapped area about the range in slopes.

To aid comprehension, brief descriptions are necessary of the soils listed in Table 4.3. In the map extract, five orders of soils according to the System of Soil Classification for Canada (Canada Soil Survey Committee, 1970) are represented, viz. chernozemic, podzolic, regosolic, brunisolic and gleysolic. The chernozemic order consists of soils, developed under xerophytic or mesophytic grasses and forbs in cool, semi-arid to subhumid climates, which have a dark-coloured surface horizon and lower horizons of high base saturation. In Fig. 4.3, such soils occur on the glaciofluvial and alluvial areas. The podzolic soils which are acidic have distinctive B horizons in which organic matter, and iron and aluminium compounds have accumulated. Regosolic soils are those which have horizon development too weak for them to be included in other orders. Soils in the brunisolic order have horizons better developed than in the regosolic order, but still lack the degrees or kinds of horizon development specified for soils of the other orders. All brunisols have a B horizon which has been chemically altered or has received some illuvial clay. Gleysols are fairly obviously developed under wet conditions to produce permanent or periodic chemical reduction, reflected in mottling and low chromas.

These soil orders are subdivided into great groups and then subgroups, and examples of the latter are given in Table 4.3. Reference must be made to the Canadian Soil Classification System for full definitions of these terms. However, it is useful to know that the term 'orthic' is used to denote the subgroup which is typical of the central concept of the great group. The map extract (Fig. 4.3) also shows areas of fractured and broken rock (R). In addition areas are mapped as talus (T) if the fractured rock material is actively moving downslope. Areas susceptible to periodic snowslides are mapped as chutes (C).

The report by Coen and Holland (1976) gives a summary of the soil characteristics for each mapping unit supplemented with profile descriptions, analytical data and colour photographs. The latter part of the report is devoted to interpreting the soil map units for selected park uses, viz. playgrounds, camping areas, trails, septic tank absorption fields, permanent buildings with and without basements, and local roads. Susceptibility to erosion was also assessed. The results from these evaluations can also be applied to related uses, for example the results from the assessment for local roads would also be applicable to car parks. Table 4.4 is an example of a guide used in the

Table 4.4 Guide for assessing soil limitations for playgrounds (From Table 3, Coen and Holland 1976, p. 82).

ITEM AFFECTING USE	DEGREE OF SOIL LIMITATION		
	None to slight	Moderate	Severe
Wetness	Rapidly, well, and moderately well drained soils; water table below 76 cm during season of use	Moderately well and imperfectly drained soils; water table below 51 cm during season of use	Imperfectly, poorly, and very poorly drained soils; water table above 51 cm during season of use
Flooding	None during season of use	May flood once in 2 yr during season of use	Floods more than once in 2 yr during season of use
Permeability	Very rapid to moderate inclusive	Moderately slow and slow	Very slow
Slope	0–2%	2–5%	5–9%
Useful moisture	Water storage capacity >13 cm and/or adequate rainfall and/or low evapotranspiration	Water storage capacity 5–13 cm and/or moderate rainfall and/or moderate evapotranspiration	Water storage capacity <5 cm and/or low rainfall and/or high evapotranspiration
Surface soil texture	SL, FSL, VFSL, L, SiL*	CL, SCL, SiCL, LS*	SC, SiC, C, S and LS* Subject to blowing, organic soils
Depth to bedrock	Over 102 cm	51–102 cm	Less than 51 cm
Coarse fragments on surface	Relatively free from fragments	Up to 20% coarse fragments	20%+ coarse fragments
Stoniness	Stones greater than 15 m apart	Stones 15–1.5 m apart	Stones less than 1.5 m apart
Rockiness	Rock exposures greater than 90 m apart and cover less than 2% of the surface	Rock exposures 90–30 m apart and cover about 2–10% of the surface	Rock exposures less than 30 m apart and cover greater than 10% of the surface

Note: This guide applies to soils to be used intensively for playgrounds for baseball, football, badminton, and other similar organized games. These areas are subject to intensive foot traffic. A nearly level surface, good drainage, and a soil texture and consistence that give a firm surface generally are required. The most desirable soils are free from rock outcrops and coarse fragments.
Soil suitability for growing and maintaining vegetation is not a part of this guide, except as influenced by moisture, but is an important item to consider in the final evaluation of site.

* sandy loam (SL), fine sandy loam (FSL), very fine sandy loam (VFSL), loam (L), silty loam (SiL), clay loam (CL), sand clay loam (SCL), sandy clay (SC), silty clay (SiC), clay (C), sand (S), loamy sand (LS), silty clay loam (SiCL).

study for assessing soil limitations – in this case the particular recreational use is playgrounds. Similar guides are given for the other selected park uses.

The results from using these guides can be demonstrated by considering the townsite of Waterton Park on the edge of the lake (Fig. 4.3). This settlement is on an alluvial fan built up by Cameron Creek supplemented by Carthew Creek. The resultant soils are coarse-textured, gravelly sandy loams developed on the low-angle alluvial fan deposits. The area is mapped as a complex of soil mapping units 21 (orthic regosol) and 22 (orthic dark brown chernozemic soils). The first soil has a thin A horizon enriched in organic matter directly overlying a C horizon which contains carbonate; the second soil is very similar to the first but has a more mature development indicated by the presence of a dark reddish-grey B horizon. The soils pose no or only slight problems in terms of septic tanks, buildings with and without basements, local roads and erosion. For playgrounds unit 21 poses serious problems due to the extent of coarse fragments on the surface and the difficulties resultant upon poor water-storage capacity. Unit 22 is in the same severe category for playgrounds, but could also occur in the moderate category if stoniness is not too severe. The degree of limitations for both soils ranges between the moderate and severe categories for camp and picnic areas. The soils pose moderate limitations to paths and trails, the main constraint being the extent of coarse fragments on the surface. A similar study in the Yoho National Park in Alberta by Coen *et al.* (1977) has also been made.

The study by Hartnup and Jarvis (1973) of the Castleford area in Yorkshire was referred to in section 4.3. Besides assessing the soils for agriculture and constructional purposes, they also considered each mapping unit in terms of suitability for woodlands, parks and gardens, golf courses and playing fields. The optimum soil texture for these uses is loam, sandy loam or silt loam. Drainage conditions should be free or moderate, though free drainage is required for playing fields. Land for playing fields must have slopes less than 1° whilst some slope variability is desirable for the other amenity uses.

In conclusion, it can be appreciated that soil surveys can yield information useful for the planning of recreational facilities. Of course, most of the limitations posed to such developments can be overcome by appropriate investment. For example, the problems presented by a high water table at a campsite could be solved by building up the ground surface by 1 m, but such an operation would be expensive. As was exemplified for urban planning in section 4.3, a soil survey is cost beneficial with regard to the planning of recreation. Areas with particular limitations can be identified and either appropriate designs made or the development can be shifted to another site without such difficulties. The soil studies in Alberta also indicate the need for relating the particular recreational activities of the area to the soil characteristics.

CHAPTER 5
THE APPLICATION OF SOIL SURVEYS IN THE NETHERLANDS

5.1 SOILS IN THE NETHERLANDS

In previous chapters emphasis has been given to the description and illustration of techniques which assist with the application of soil data to land use planning. Examples have been selected from several countries, but the result is that no assessment of the success of applied soil survey in any one country has been possible. In this penultimate chapter, the Netherlands are taken as a case study in order to demonstrate how a range of techniques is used to aid land use planning. Little reference has been made to Dutch work in earlier chapters, but this in no way implies a lack in the application of soil survey research. Indeed, as will quickly become apparent, the Dutch are extremely active in applying the results of soil surveys, and this high degree of involvement of soil surveyors with planning can be viewed as the situation to which other countries ought to aspire, an objective applicable to Britain. Hartnup (1976), in reviewing the use of soil surveys in Britain and the Netherlands, concludes that soil survey information could be used much more widely in Britain. Before attention is focused on the application of soil survey data, consideration must be given to the nature of soils in the Netherlands.

The country is extensively mantled with Pleistocene and Holocene deposits and over 99 per cent of the Netherlands has soils derived from these materials. Only in the south of Limburg are there instances of soils developed directly on older formations (Cretaceous chalk) though usually these rocks are mantled with loess. Given the small size of the country and the lack of much altitudinal variation, the climate tends to be comparatively uniform. Differences in soils are closely associated with variations in parent material, drainage conditions and the effect of man through land reclamation, agriculture and soil improvement. Dominance should be given to parent material and its origin since these strongly influence the nature of soils. Figure 5.1 shows the distribution of soils according to parent material for the whole country whilst Fig. 5.2 is an extract from a 1:200 000 soil map and shows the soils in the area to the immediate west of Arnhem and Nijmegen. The following description should aid an understanding of soils throughout the Netherlands (Fig. 5.1) as well as for the sample area at 1:200 000 (Fig. 5.2 and Table 5.1). The information about soils is extracted from the *Atlas van Nederland* (1963–77) and from the *Major soils and soil regions in the Netherlands* by de Bakker (1979).

1. Marine-clay soils

These clays, of Holocene age, cover about a quarter of the country and de Bakker (1979) subdivides the marine districts into four regions

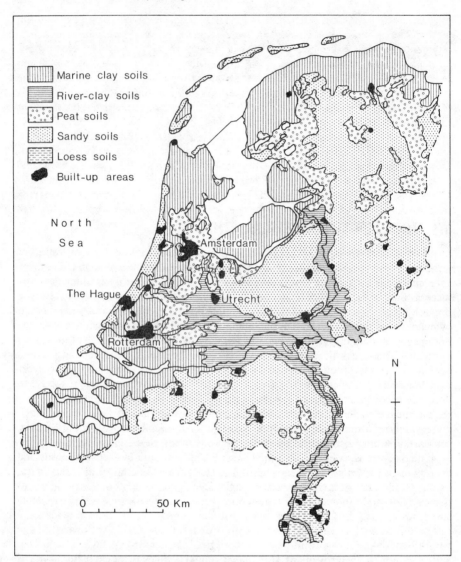

Fig. 5.1   General soil map of the Netherlands (From Van Dam and Zegers, 1977).

(a) The bottomlands in the drained lakes: This area occurs below the 2.5 m contour in the west of the country from around Amsterdam to Rotterdam and The Hague. As can be seen from Fig. 5.1, the area is an intricate pattern of marine-clay soils and peat. Prior to the beginning of reclamation in the tenth century, this area was a fenland. Ditches were dug to improve drainage, but a consequence was also the shrinkage of the peat resulting in shallow lakes, also formed by the cutting of peat. These lakes began to be reclaimed during the sixteenth century to produce small polders with soils developed on marine clays.

(b) Coastal polders: These coastal polders were areas of tidal marsh which have been reclaimed; the period of greatest activity was from AD 1600 to 1625 when 32 000 ha

were created (de Bakker, 1979). The description associated with the 1 : 200 000 soil map describes most of the soils on these polders as young sea-clay soils since sedimentation has taken place since Roman times.

(c) Older reclaimed marine clays: This region lies between 1 m below and 0.5 m above sea level and the clays thin out eastwards over peat, alluvium or Pleistocene sands. These clays were deposited before the clays of the coastal polders with the upper sediment dating to between 1500 BC and AD 1100. The land on these marine clays was thus enclosed before the coastal polders.

(d) The Zuider Zee polders: The Zuider Zee was a shallow marine lake which was enclosed in 1932 to create Lake Yssel. Four polders have been reclaimed, viz. Wieringermeer (drained 1930), North Eastern Polder (1942), Eastern Flevoland (1957), South Flevoland (1968) and Markerwaard is due to be drained in the early 1980s. The material on the floor of the original Zuider Zee is not restricted to clay; in the centre clay is dominant, but on the borders clayey sand and fine sand also occur. All these sediments are calcareous.

2. River-clay soils

River sediments deposited by the Rhine and Meuse during the Holocene cover almost 8 per cent of the country (de Bakker, 1979). Such materials have been deposited by meandering rivers. It should not be thought that sediments are dominated by clays. For example, coarser textured material with a coarse sand subsoil is found on levees. Other components of the floodplains are the forelands (between the levees and the edge of the floodplain). Sediments high in clay content are common in backswamps. The intricacies of alluvial history will be illustrated when the soils in Fig. 5.2 are described.

3. Peat soils

Peat soils cover about 13 per cent of the Netherlands and occur on the landward side of the marine clays (Fig. 5.1). A marine regression followed the deposition of the clays, giving a marshy lagoonal environment. Peat began to develop over the tidal swamps, first as reed swamp and ultimately with the growth of sphagnum resulting in raised bogs. Such peat provided an excellent source of fuel and the eventual result was man-made lakes, some of which were later reclaimed as polders on the underlying marine clay. Figure 5.1 also shows peat areas within the sandy soils, the most extensive example being in the extreme north-east of the country. Again, these peats have been extensively cut.

4. Sandy soils

Soils derived from sands cover about 40 per cent of the Netherlands and four types of region can be identified.

(a) Ice-pushed ridges: During the early part of the Pleistocene much coarse-textured alluvium was deposited by the rivers Rhine and Meuse. This alluvium was subjected to massive thrusting by the Saale ice-sheet, thus producing ice-pushed ridges. As an example, the area known as the Veluwe to the north of Arnhem is distinctly hilly by Dutch standards because it is composed of these sandy and gravelly ice-pushed ridges. Coarse sands and gravels were also deposited by glaciofluvial processes.

(d) Coversands: During the last major glaciation (the Weichsel), the Netherlands was ice free, but the tundra conditions of the time permitted very active aeolian processes. Fine and loamy fine sand were picked up, transported and deposited as material called 'coversand' which is thickest in valleys and also lies on or against ice-pushed ridges or glaciofluvial deposits.

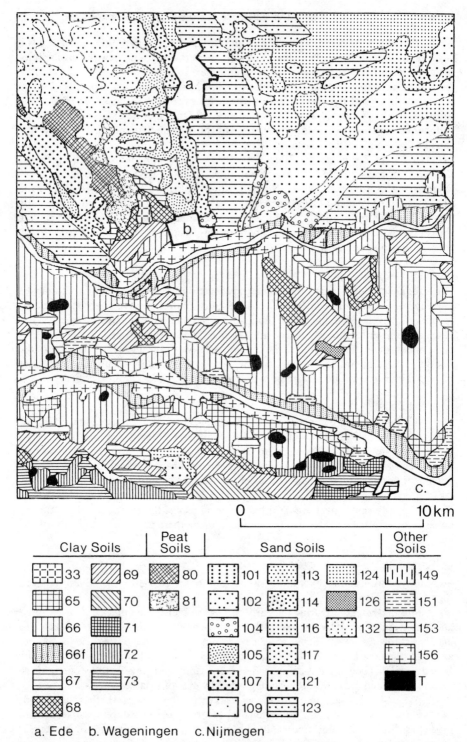

Clay Soils		Peat Soils	Sand Soils			Other Soils
33	69	80	101	113	124	149
65	70	81	102	114	126	151
66	71		104	116	132	153
66f	72		105	117		156
67	73		107	121		T
68			109	123		

a. Ede   b. Wageningen   c. Nijmegen

Fig. 5.2 Soils in the vicinity of Wageningen, Gelderland, the Netherlands (From *Soil Map of Gelderland 1 : 200 000*, Plate IV 4, 1960, published also in *Atlas van Nederland*). The legend is provided in Table 5.1.

Table 5.1 Legend to Fig. 5.2 (Extracted from the legend to the 1:200 000 soil maps of the Netherlands, *Atlas van Nederland*, Plate IV 11).

Young sea-clay soil	Non-calcareous, peat beginning between 40 and 80 cm, occasionally between 80 and 120 cm			Heavy clay	33
Younger river-clay soils	Calcareous and slightly calcareous, occasional shallow non-calcareous	Association: medium and high	Becoming lighter with depth or homogeneous	Clayey sand and very sandy clay	65
				Moderately sandy and light clay	66
				As 66, but liable to flood	66f
			Subsoil of non-calcareous heavy clay	Sandy and light clay	67
	Non-calcareous, occasionally slightly calcareous below 50 cm	Association: low and medium high	Becoming lighter with depth, heavy clay		68
			Homogeneous, heavy clay		69
			Association of heavy clay overlying old river clay		70
		Association: medium high and high	Becoming lighter with depth or homogeneous	Clayey sand and very sandy clay	71
				Moderately sandy and light clay	72

Table 5.1 *(continued)*

Peat soils	Low-moor peat, not cut over		Subsoil of non-calcareous heavy clay	Sandy and light clay	73
			Overlying sphagnum moss peat or sedge peat	Clay-poor, clayey and sandy clayey peat	80
				Peaty and humus-rich clay and sandy clay	81
Sand soils	Non-calcareous	Low	Humus podzols; very poor sand	Non-loamy and slightly loamy	101
			Gley soils; very poor sand	Loamy fine sand	102
		Medium high	Old arable land; very poor sand	Slightly loamy	104
				Slightly loamy	105
			Podzols; very poor sand	Non-loamy fine sand	107
				Slightly loamy	109
		High	Old arable land; very poor sand	Slightly loamy	113
				Slightly loamy	114

Table 5.1 (continued)

Category	Group / Association	Description	Texture	No.
		Podzols; very poor sand	Non-loamy fine sand	116
			Non-loamy and slightly loamy coarse sand	117
		Podzols; predominantly poor sand	Non-loamy	121
			Ice-pushed ridges; gravelly non-loamy and loamy sand	123
		Humus-poor; poor and very poor sand	Non-loamy	124
	Association: medium high and high	Brown, old arable land; poor sand	Loamy	126
	Associations of sand, loam, river clay and peat soils	Association of valley bottom soils	Non-loamy and loamy fine sand, peat	132
	Association: high	Slope-complex; coarse sandy gravel soils		149
'Loam' soil	Association of 'loam', sand and older clay soil			151
Miscellaneous soils	Calcareous and slightly calcareous; humus-poor and shallowly humose	Lighter with depth; clayey and clay-poor fine and coarse sand		153
	Non-calcareous; humus-poor to strongly humose	Complex: low and medium high, occasionally high; sand to clay		156
	Complex: excavated and/or raised by suction-dredging for over 50% of the area			
	Terpen: old settlement sites; dark soils, occasionally raised			T

(c) Coversands over glacial till: The effect of the Saale glaciation was also to veneer parts of the country with glacial till which was subsequently mantled by coversands.
(d) Holocene sands: In this category must be mentioned the coastal dune belt; marine sands in parts of the former Zuider Zee and the inland dunes which have formed in historical times.

5. Loess soils

Loess has exactly the same origin and age as the coversands, but is better sorted and occurs in the particle size range 10–50 μm (dominantly silt). It only covers about 2 per cent of the country and occurs in the southern part of Limburg as well as in the lee of ice-pushed ridges, for example in the regions of Arnhem and Nijmegen. Vink (1949) carried out research on the nature of loess and coversands with specific reference to the south-eastern part of the Veluwe.

Figure 5.2 includes examples of soils derived from all these types of parent materials with the exception of loess. The map and the associated legend (Table 5.1) merit careful study since many of the attributes of Dutch soils can be introduced. The map is an extract from Plate IV, 4 of the *Atlas van Nederland* (1963–77) which includes all the 1 : 200 000 soil maps. For these maps a system of soil classification had to be developed; soils are first subdivided into broad parent material groups and then according to profile characteristics. Some idea of the classification scheme can be obtained from Table 5.1 which only includes mapping units within the map extract (Fig. 5.2). Before the nature of the individual mapping units is described, a brief comment needs to be made about soils being described as 'high', 'medium' or 'low'. Low soils are strongly influenced by groundwater, whilst high soils are developed in the absence of groundwater influence. Clearly, medium soils are in an intermediate position. An association is a mapping unit combining a number of soil units together, and these component units could be separated on a larger scale map. A complex is the same as an association except that it is not possible to separate soil units on a more detailed map.

There is only one mapping unit within the map extract of a sea-clay soil (33) – a sticky heavy clay overlying peat. There is a range of younger river-clay soils along the Rhine, Waal and Maas. These sediments were deposited during the Holocene by meandering rivers. The soils on the Rhine alluvium are medium and high in relation to groundwater and are calcareous (65, 66 and 67) in contrast to the non-calcareous soils of the Maas system. Soils on levees tend to be above the influence of groundwater though they vary in texture. For example river discharge increased during the ninth and tenth centuries resulting in very light textured levees (65, 71); these levees lie on the river side of the older levees with a higher clay content (66, 72). The meandering nature of the rivers has meant many changes in channels; for example levees can overlie basin clay (67, 73). The opposite is also possible where basin clay overlies lighter texture material (68). Basin clays (69) occur between levees and the limit of the floodplains and these heavy soils stand out in contrast to the levees. However, in the western part of Gelderland, the rivers begin to be tidal causing levees to be poorly developed and often heavy textured (66). Since the thirteenth and fourteenth centuries, the rivers have been constrained by dykes with flooding being usually limited to map unit 66f. Ruptures of these dykes have occurred resulting in deposition in fan shapes at the breaches (151). The river clays have been excavated for brick manufacture (156).

Another wide range of soils are developed on sands which occur to the north of the Rhine. In this area there are also localised examples of peat soils (80, 81). As already mentioned, the rivers deposited extensive sand prior to the Saale glaciation. These sands are described as poor since they have lost many minerals through weathering. Very poor sand consists solely of quartz. Much of this material was pushed by the ice into ridges on which humus iron podzols (123) have developed. There are also instances of these pre-Saalian sands which have not been pushed (101, 107 and 116) and on which humus podzols or podzols are located. Podzols also occur on glaciofluvial deposits (121). Coversands also mantle the older sands, reflected in the non-loamy fine sand texture of mapping unit 116. Inland dunes are also represented in mapping unit 124; these soils exhibit negligible formation. Variations in water-table conditions are apparent within the sand area from humus podzols (101) and gley soils (102) in depressional localities to soils described as medium and high which are further removed in a vertical sense from the influence of goundwater.

Within the sand soils group, there are examples of 'old arable land' (104, 105, 113, 114 and 126). These are man-made or anthropogenic soils, often called plaggen soils. In Dutch and German 'plaggen' means turves; these soils were built up over the centuries by cutting turves which were used for bedding material in cowsheds and sheepfolds and subsequently added to surrounding fields as dung (de Bakker, 1979). The heathlands on the coarse sands were extensively used as a source of heather turves which when used on the arable land produced black plaggen soils. These gradually built up, often to the order of about 1 m above the surrounding soils. Such an elevation would have taken of the order of 750 years to develop (de Bakker, 1979, quoting the work of Staring). The cutting of grass turves resulted in brown plaggen soils (126).

The cutting of turves, especially on the heathlands, as well as the effect of sheep grazing and occasional fires, encouraged soil erosion. In certain areas, sand dunes formed which buried arable land. Most of these inland sand dunes have been stabilised by afforestation, but soils on this blown sand are very poorly developed (124). Soils were also formed and built up by the action of human habitation, a process similar to tell formation in the eastern Mediterranean and Middle East, albeit on a lesser scale (Davidson, 1976c). These old settlement sites are called 'terpen' and are indicated by the mapping unit T on Fig. 5.2. As would be expected, these sites tend to be associated with the slightly higher and better drained localities in the river clay area.

Description of the soils in the Wageningen area (Fig. 5.2) has introduced many of the characteristics of Dutch soils, with the major exception of the marine-clay area which is hardly represented. As already stated, Fig. 5.2 is an extract of a 1 : 200 000 soil map and soil maps are available at this scale for the whole country. The Netherlands Soil Survey Institute is in the process of publishing maps at a scale of 1 : 50 000 and about 60 per cent of the country is covered at this scale; the Lake Yssel Development Authority has the task of mapping the soils in the polders of the former Zuider Zee. Soil maps at a scale of 1 : 25 000 or 1 : 10 000 are also published, though these are usually commissioned surveys (Haans, 1975).

5.2 SOIL SURVEY INTERPRETATION

The Dutch landscape is well known for its intensity of use and land is under ever increasing pressure. Not only is there need to preserve as far as possible the soils most suitable for agriculture which plays an important role in the Dutch economy, but space must also be found for new houses, industrial areas, recreational areas, forestry and roads. The application of soil survey in the 1950s is summarised by Edelman (1963) who describes the use of such research primarily for crop production and for land reclamation and improvement. He gives brief consideration to soil surveys in relation to town and country planning with the main contribution in the Netherlands being the preservation of soils particularly suitable for horticulture. In the review of soil survey application by Haans and Wesherveld (1970), the marked rise in the use of soil data in the non-agricultural sector is noted. Such applications will be described later in this chapter, but it seems appropriate to begin with illustrating how soil survey information can be interpreted for particular agricultural purposes.

The 1 : 200 000 soil maps have been the basis for an assessment of soil suitability, for arable land and grassland. Details of the scheme are provided in English by Vink and van Zuilen (1974) with a summary also in Vink (1975). The first 1 : 200 000 soil map was completed in 1961, and even before that time the need for a general assessment of the country's soils for agriculture had been identified. An early report on the suitability scheme is given by Vink (1963b). Soil suitability is defined as 'the degree of success with which a crop or range of crops can be regularly grown on a certain soil, within the existing type of farming, under good management, and under good conditions of parcellation and accessibility' (Vink and van Zuilen, 1974, p. 17). The assessment is made on a qualitative basis with reference to the economic and technological situation of agriculture about 1960. Thus, as with the USDA land use capability scheme (Ch. 2), various assumptions are necessary before land or soil grading is possible. Changes in these assumptions, resultant for example upon the introduction of a new farming layout or new machinery which can cope with difficult soils, mean that the suitability assessments ought to be reappraised.

The suitability system recognises five major classes:

Major class BG	Soils generally suited to arable land and usually also to grassland.
Major class GB	Soils generally suited to grassland and in many cases also to arable land.
Major class B	Soils generally suited to arable land, but mostly poorly or not suited to grassland.
Major class G	Soils generally suited to grassland, but mostly poorly or not suited to arable land.
Major class O	Soils predominantly poorly suited to arable land and to grassland.

Each of these major classes is subdivided into a number of classes on the basis of crop flexibility; in the case of grassland soils (major class G), emphasis is given to their gross production, distribution of grass growth throughout the growing season, the bearing capacity of the sod and the fodder quality. Descriptions of the classes are given in Appendix 3. Application of this method has made possible the assignment of all the soil mapping units of the 1 : 200 000 *Soil map of the Netherlands* to particular soil suitability classes. Figure 5.3 shows the distribution of soil suitability classes for the same area as Fig. 5.2. As can be seen much of the high podzols on the sand area to the east of a line between Wageningen and Ede are in class B3 – arable land soils of extremely limited suitability. The inland dunes (124) support unsuitable soils because of their dry nature (class 01). Much of the area between the Rhine and the Waal is assessed as arable land and grassland soils of wide suitability (class BG2a), though on soils dominated by heavy clay (mapping unit 69), the evaluation is for a grassland and arable land complex of limited suitability (GB3).

The overall objective of this suitability scheme was to indicate the degree of agricultural success which could be expected from management of the different soils under specified conditions. The results are necessarily fairly generalised, given the scale of mapping, and have been used primarily for land use strategic planning. More detailed planning requires evaluation of the 1 : 50 000 or larger scale soil maps. One

Fig. 5.3 Soil suitability for arable land and grassland in the same area as in Fig. 5.2. See Appendix 3 for detailed legend (From Vink and Van Zuilen, 1974, opposite p. 36).

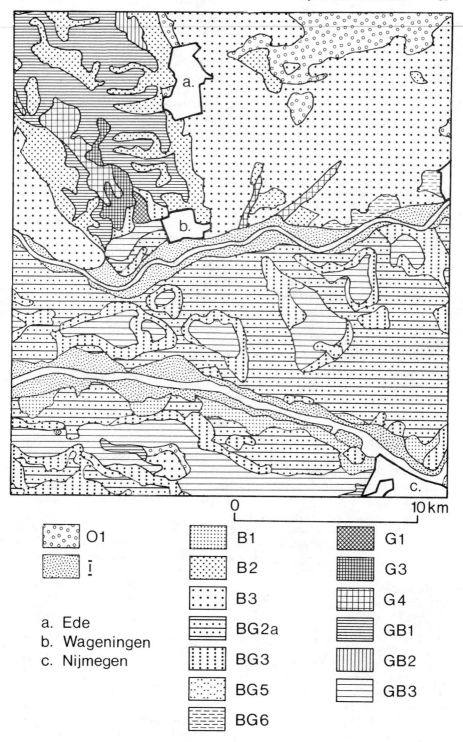

0   10 km

O1	B1	G1
Ī	B2	G3
	B3	G4
a. Ede	BG2a	GB1
b. Wageningen	BG3	GB2
c. Nijmegen	BG5	GB3
	BG6	

disadvantage of the results when only presented in a form similar to Fig. 5.3, is that the map user is given no information as to why specific soils have been allocated to particular classes, a problem raised by Haans and Westerveld (1970). For planning purposes it is often useful to have a table indicating the limitations associated with each soil. Such a table can easily be produced when the basic soil map is at a more detailed scale.

The interpretation of larger scale soil maps for land use planning purposes can be illustrated by an extract from a 1 : 25 000 map. Dekkers, Zegers and Westerveld (1972) demonstrate how the 1 : 25 000 soil map for the area of Brouwhuis to the immediate south-east of Helmond can assist with the structure-plan for Helmond. As can be seen from Fig. 5.4a, the soils are derived from non-calcareous sands. The soils are classified using a different classification system to the 1 : 200 000 *Soil map of the Netherlands*. This system is fully specified by de Bakker and Schelling (1966), but for present purposes mention need only be made of the soil mapping units on Fig. 5.4a. Three types of podzols are present and these vary in texture and thickness of topsoil. 'Enk' earth soils are plaggen soils and have thick topsoils. 'Beek' earth soils display hydromorphic characteristics – for example a non-aerated subsoil within a depth of 80 cm. Mapping unit 102 (a gley soil) on Fig. 5.2 is an example of a 'beek' earth soil. The fact that 'vague' soils are associated with inland dunes should make their nature clear.

Soil maps at the scale of 1 : 50 000 and 1 : 25 000 also show water-table classes, but information has been excluded from Fig. 5.4a since it is given in Fig. 5.4b. The depth and fluctuation of the water table are of marked practical importance and the water-table classes are defined in the key to Fig. 5.4b.

Figures 5.4c, d, e and f illustrate the interpretation of basic soil survey data for different land uses. As can be seen, the soils are assessed in the first instance as high, moderately or poorly suitable for the particular land uses. These three categories are further subdivided according to degree of suitability, with information also being given on the type of particular limitations as well as an indication as to whether such limitations are moderate or severe. The study by Dekkers, Zegers and Westerveld

Table 5.2 Assessment factors and their use for various land use forms in the Netherlands (From Haans, 1978).

ASSESSMENT FACTOR	LAND USE FORM				
	Arable farming	Grassland farming	Forestry	Recreational land use	Low rise development
Drainage status	+	+	+	+	+
Moisture supply capacity	+	+	+	+	
Bearing capacity topsoil		+		+	
Workability	+				
Structural stability	+				
Bearing capacity subsoil					+
Fertility status			+		

Fig. 5.4 Soil and soil suitability maps for the vicinity of Brouwhuis: (a) soil map; (b) groundwater table map; (c) suitability for arable land; (d) suitability for pasture; (e) suitability for grass sportsfields; (f) suitability for building construction. (From Dekkers, Zegers and Westerveld, 1972).

SOILS   (a)

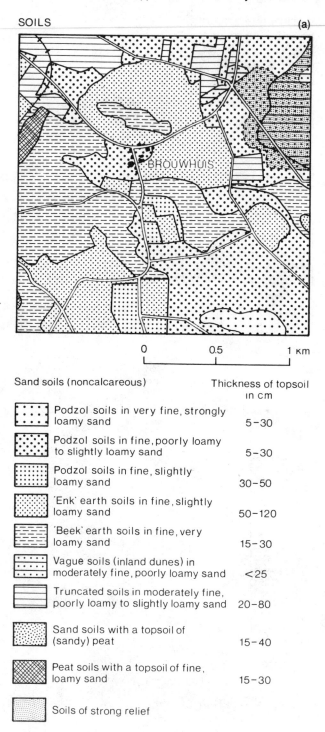

0   0.5   1 κm

Sand soils (noncalcareous)   Thickness of topsoil
                                                    in cm

Podzol soils in very fine, strongly
loamy sand   5 – 30

Podzol soils in fine, poorly loamy
to slightly loamy sand   5 – 30

Podzol soils in fine, slightly
loamy sand   30 – 50

'Enk' earth soils in fine, slightly
loamy sand   50 – 120

'Beek' earth soils in fine, very
loamy sand   15 – 30

Vague soils (inland dunes) in
moderately fine, poorly loamy sand   < 25

Truncated soils in moderately fine,
poorly loamy to slightly loamy sand   20 – 80

Sand soils with a topsoil of
(sandy) peat   15 – 40

Peat soils with a topsoil of fine,
loamy sand   15 – 30

Soils of strong relief

WATER–TABLE CLASSES   (b)

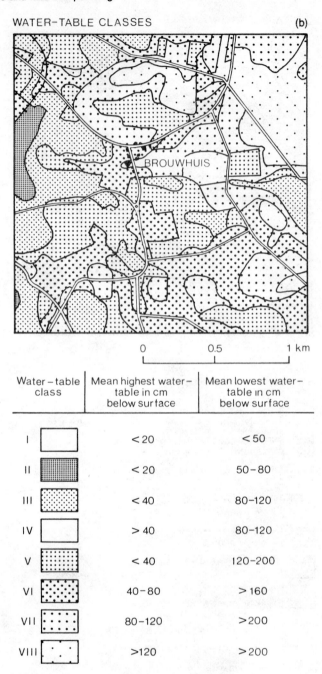

Water–table class		Mean highest water– table in cm below surface	Mean lowest water– table in cm below surface
I		< 20	< 50
II		< 20	50–80
III		< 40	80–120
IV		> 40	80–120
V		< 40	120–200
VI		40–80	> 160
VII		80–120	> 200
VIII		> 120	> 200

Water–table classes I & IV do not occur in this area

SUITABILITY FOR ARABLE   (c)

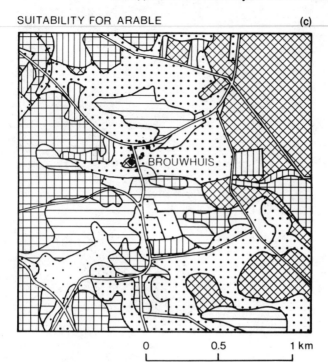

Highly suitable soils

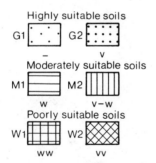

G1   [· ·]   G2   [: : :]
       –   v
Moderately suitable soils

M1 [≡]   M2 [|||]
     w   v–w
Poorly suitable soils

W1 [⊞]   W2 [⧈]
    ww   vv

G1 ──▶ G2 : decreasing suitability in class G

Limitations

None/slight	Moderate	Severe	Description
–	v	vv	moisture deficiency
–	w	ww	excess of water

SUITABILITY FOR PASTURE   (d)

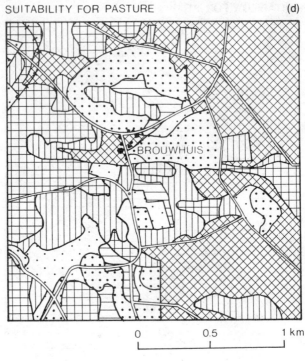

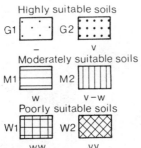

Highly suitable soils

G1 [. .]   G2 [::]
        –   v

Moderately suitable soils

M1 [≡]   M2 [|||]
       w   v – w

Poorly suitable soils

W1 [▦]   W2 [▨]
      ww   vv

G1 ——▶ G2 : decreasing suitability in class G

Limitations

None/slight	Moderate	Severe	Description
–	v	vv	moisture deficiency
–	w	ww	excess of water

SUITABILITY FOR GRASS SPORTSFIELDS   (e)

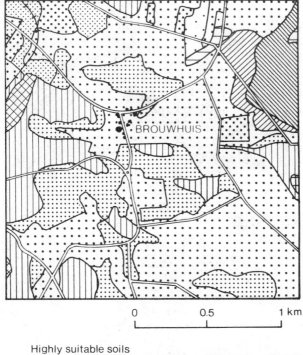

BROUWHUIS

0   0.5   1 km

Highly suitable soils

G1 · · ·   G2 : : :   G3 (w)   G4 (l-w)   G5 (ww)

Moderately suitable soils

M1 (aa)   M2 (ll-ww)   M3 (a-rr)   M4 (aa-rr)

Poorly suitable soils

W1 (p-ll-ww)   W2 (pp-ll-ww)

G1 ——▶ G5 : decreasing suitability in class G

Limitations

None/slight	Moderate	Severe	Description
–	a	aa	topsoil too thin
–	l	ll	too much organic matter and/or loam in topsoil
–	p	pp	unfavourable horizon sequence
–	w	ww	excess of water
–	–	rr	too much relief

SUITABILITY FOR BUILDING CONSTRUCTION   (f)

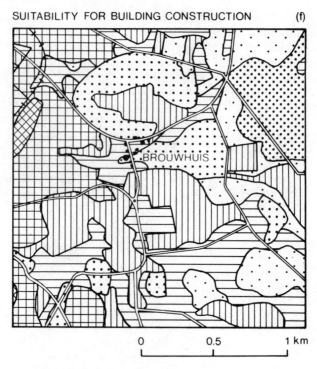

0   0.5   1 km

Highly suitable soils

G1   G2   G3
 –   h   rr

Moderately suitable soils

M1   M2
 w   ww

Poorly suitable soils

W1   W2
dd – ww   dd – h – ww

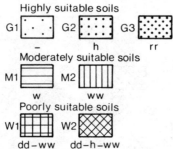

G1 ➝ G3 :decreasing suitability in class G

Limitations

None/slight	Moderate	Severe	Description
–	–	dd	bearing capacity of subsoil inadequate
–	h	–	topsoil too thick
–	w	ww	excess of water
–	–	rr	too much relief

(1972) also provides other suitability assessments as well as a table summarising the suitability and limitations of each soil and water-table mapping unit.

The preceding description of Figs 5.4(c), (d), (e) and (f) in no way considered how the soils were evaluated for the different land uses. Fairly clearly, the soil conditions had to be evaluated with reference to the requirements of the particular uses. Haans and van Lynden (1978) and Haans (1978) stress the importance of assessment factors in the execution of this task. These are particular combinations of soil properties relevant to specific land uses. Table 5.2 lists seven assessment factors and indicates their varying relevance to five land uses. Fertility status rather surprisingly is only relevant to forestry, the argument being that differences in natural fertility for arable and grassland farming can easily be corrected by application of fertilizers. These assessment factors are usually divided into five classes; an example is the subdivision of the assessment factor drainage status according to mean highest groundwater depth. Haans (1978) defines the classes as follows:

CLASS	MEAN HIGHEST GROUNDWATER DEPTH BELOW SURVACE (cm)
1	> 80
2	40–80
3	25–40
4	15–25
5	< 15

The next step is a comparison of specific land use requirements with the classes of the assessment factors. For example, the significance of these various drainage status classes could be assessed with reference to arable farming or to specific crops. This is usually achieved by informal procedures based on experience and empirical research. Some combination of classes would usually be possible and then groupings of classes from several assessment factors would define overall suitability classes (highly, moderately and poorly suited as in Fig 5.4 (c), (d), (e) (f) which may be further subdivided. The stages in the interpretation of soil maps following this Dutch method are summarised in Fig. 5.5

5.3 SOIL INTERPRETATION FOR SPECIAL PURPOSES

Horticulture has for long been an important economic activity and occupies 5.5 per cent of the total land area (de Bakker, 1979). In the Netherlands some of the earliest work on soil assessment was done with specific reference to horticultural crops. Edelman (1963) describes work by Van Liere (1948) who investigated the effect of soil conditions on the root systems of vines grown in greenhouses. Crop yields are of course related to root systems, and Van Liere revealed major differences in yields between soil units in the Westland area. He also found that, other things being equal, grapes from the most productive soils fetched higher prices than those from poor-quality soils because grapes from the former soils are more suitable for cold storage.

The success of orchards in the Netherlands can in part be related to soil conditions. The incidence of poor patches in orchards has been investigated by de Bakker (1950) who has demonstrated the effect of a coarse sandy subsoil on tree growth and thus on yield. Soil limitations to orchards can be compensated by varying the distance between

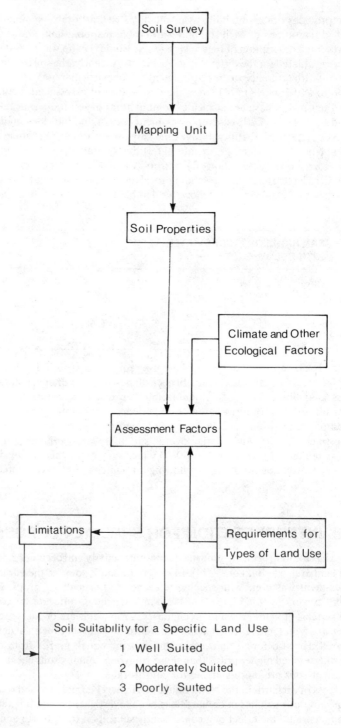

Fig. 5.5 Stages in the interpretation of soil maps (From Haans, 1978).

trees (Van Dam, 1973). The yield and quality of asparagus spears are strongly influenced by soil type (Haans and Westerveld, 1970; Van Dam, 1973) with the best yield and quality coming from high 'enk' earth soils (plaggen soils well above the water table). A sandy soil is also highly desirable so that the soil can be easily removed to harvest the white shoots.

The effect of soils on tomatoes grown in heated greenhouses at first may not be very obvious, but Haans and Westerveld (1970) and Van Dam (1973) report a clear correlation between soil conditions and earliness of harvest. The earliness of yield depends upon the number of fruits in the first trusses and the early setting of fruit is encouraged on clay soils. According to Van Dam (1973), tomato plants on clay soils have greater difficulty in obtaining water than if they were grown on sandy soils because of the strong soil-moisture retention and low conductivity of clays. The results on clay soils are stronger tomato plants which have greater success at early fruit-set. There are clear financial advantages in producing tomatoes as early as possible, also influenced of course by the level of heating in the greenhouses. The results of growing tomatoes in experimental plots on different soils showed, in contrast to asparagus, no clear correlation between soil type and yield. However, there are distinct management advantages of locating greenhouses such that there is homogeneity of soils within them.

In terms of selecting suitable soils for horticulture, soil conditions seem more relevant to field crops. For indoor crops, systems of management can be selected appropriate to the soils, though as was shown with tomatoes the nature of the soil type can influence crop earliness and thus financial returns.

Urban development

The Dutch have always attached great importance to the selection of sites for settlements; the early sites, for example in the river-clay area (Fig. 5.2), were located on the higher and drier river levee soils. Such soils offered sites which were not liable to flood and had good bearing capacities. Today urban planners have still to take account of the nature of soils in areas proposed for urban development. For example, construction on wet clay or peat soils requires the provision of 1–2 m of sand over the area before work can begin, an operation which is expensive. The resultant urban landscape tends to be bleak and harsh (Westerveld and van den Hurk, 1973). Thus besides there being a distinct cost advantage of a soil survey prior to urban development, there is also the chance of a much better integration of the urban landscape with the natural one. For example localised occurrences of wet clay soils instead of being mantled with sand, could provide public open space, or be designed for wildlife.

Figure 5.4 (f) illustrates how a soil survey can be interpreted for constructional purposes. A similar approach is also exemplified by Westerveld and van den Hurk (1973) who consider the area around Utrecht. In terms of soil interpretation for building purposes, prime importance was given to groundwater level and bearing capacity. For building in the Utrecht area, it was considered essential that the groundwater was more than 1 m below the surface; this required 1 m of elevating material for sand and clay soils which did not meet this drainage condition and 1.5 m for peat soils. Bearing capacity was closely related to the depth of underlying Pleistocene sand. Thus it was possible to calculate the total costs per mapping unit necessary to make the soils suitable for buildings. It was found that the costs of making peat soils suitable for building could be twice as high as preparing sand soils. Quite clearly, maps showing such variations in costs can be of great assistance in the planning of urban areas.

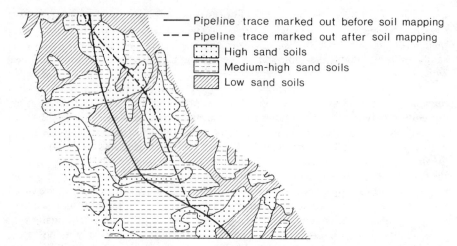

Fig. 5.6   Route for a gas pipeline, planned with and without the aid of a soil map (From Haans and Westerveld, 1970, p. 307).

Engineering applications

The interpretation of soil survey information is applicable to engineering in a similar way to urban planning. In other words, certain specific problems and associated costs can be anticipated at an earlier stage if a soil survey has been carried out. This can be demonstrated for engineering by considering the selection of a pipeline route (Fig. 5.6). This example, as described by Haans and Westerveld (1970), shows how a change in route would allow the pipeline to avoid an area of low sands; these are soils which are very much dominated by a high water table. Information about water-table regime and bearing capacity aids not only the selection of the route but also the timing of construction and the techniques used.

Recreation

The high density of population combined with a high standard of living generates intensive recreational pressure in the Netherlands. In the 1950s only 4 m² of recreational space was available per person within 10 km of Rotterdam (Van Onzenoort, 1973). As with all types of land use planning, there are many considerations in the design and provision of recreational areas, a topic reviewed for rural areas in the Netherlands by Van Lier (1972) and summarised by Vink (1975). In essence Van Lier (1972) identifies three groups of problems which require to be solved for recreational planning, viz. locational, capacity and layout problems. Soil information can assist with locating suitable areas, with predicting the maximum intensity of use without damage and with designing the layout of the facilities. These applications of soil information can be illustrated and amplified for the planning of grass sportsfields by summarising the report by Van Dam and Zegers (1977).

The results of a soil survey can be interpreted with respect to grass sportsfields if information is available on the soil requirements of sportsfields. Figure 5.4e shows the interpretation of the soil map (Fig. 5.4a) for sportsfields. As can be seen the high 'enk' earth soils are highly suitable based on the good drainage conditions and ability to support a good sward. At the other extreme poorly drained peat soils with a topsoil of fine loamy sand are assessed as being poorly suitable for sportsfields. Thus a soil map can help with the location of suitable areas for sportsfields. Once a location is selected, a

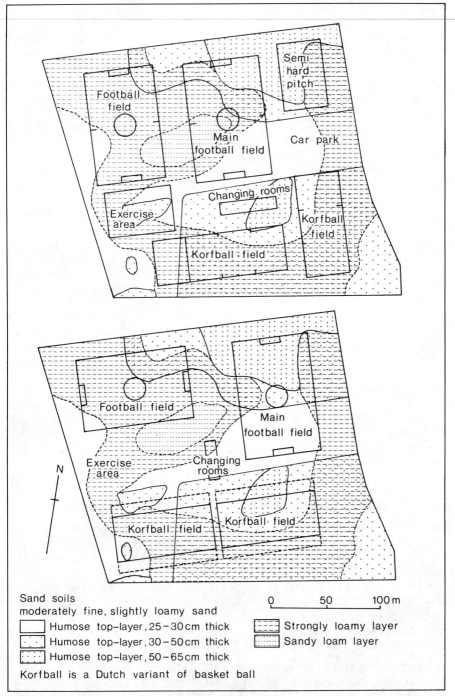

Sand soils
moderately fine, slightly loamy sand

☐ Humose top-layer, 25–30 cm thick
⬚ Humose top-layer, 30–50 cm thick
⬚ Humose top-layer, 50–65 cm thick

Korfball is a Dutch variant of basket ball

0   50   100 m

▦ Strongly loamy layer
▦ Sandy loam layer

Fig. 5.7 An example of how a soil survey can aid the planning of a sportsfield. The design in the upper diagram takes no account of soil conditions. The design in the lower diagram has been modified according to soil conditions (From van Dam and Zegers, 1977).

more intensive soil survey (scale 1 : 1 000 or 1 : 2 000) can aid the detailed layout of the recreational facilities. Besides detailed observations on soil and water-table characteristics, measures of permeability may also be made. The advantages of using the results from such a soil survey are clear from Fig. 5.7. The upper part of the figure shows the layout plan without reference to soil types whilst the lower figure illustrates the changes in design as a result of soil considerations. As can be seen, the area has soils of varying thickness and texture. It needs to be mentioned that in the Dutch system of soil classification, 'loam' refers to the particle size range less than 0.05 mm, whilst the term 'humose' refers to an organic matter class. In the revised plan, the main football field is relocated to minimise the area on the slowly permeable loamy layer. An additional advantage is that the main field is dominantly sited on soil with a thick humic topsoil thus reducing the chance of the sward drying out in the summer. Once sportsfields are established, soil information is also of value for aiding management and for planning improvement measures, for example drainage. In fact Van Dam and Zegers (1977) report that the Netherlands Soil Survey Institute has surveyed various sportsfields so that soil improvement measures could be introduced.

For recreational planning, mention must also be made of the use of soil information when dealing with reclaimed land. The South Flevoland polder is within 20 km of Amsterdam and is thus subject to intensive recreational pressure. Many recreational areas have been laid out and soil information has been helpful in their planning. Another polder near Amsterdam in part being reclaimed for recreation is 'Twiskepolder' to the immediate north of the city. This area was covered by peat which was cut as a fuel prior to 1940 (Westerveld and van den Hurk, 1973). In 1943 a dyke was built to enclose the area and drainage was then possible. The southern part began to be used as grassland whilst the remainder was peat marshland and irregular pools. An artificial lake was formed as a result of the extraction of sand which occurs beneath the peat. On completion of sand extraction, the area was to be reclaimed for recreation with a range of facilities from yachting, grassed playgrounds, and forest walks to an area of peat marsh retained as a nature reserve. Westerveld and van den Hurk (1973) provide maps showing the financial investments required per soil mapping unit to make soils suitable for deciduous trees and for grassed playgrounds and picnic areas. Again, this is an example of detailed applied soil survey work as carried out in the Netherlands.

5.4 LAND RECLAMATION AND RURAL DEVELOPMENT

No chapter on the Netherlands would be complete without discussion of their land reclamation and rural development schemes, all of which depend on a contribution from soil survey work. The role of soil survey can first be demonstrated with reference to the reclamation in the former Zuider Zee.

It is beyond the scope of the present discussion to describe in detail the planning of these polders; a succinct account is provided by Smits (n.d). For present purposes a brief outline is necessary before attention is focused on the various applications of soil survey work. Excluding the research and planning stages, the steps involved in the drainage and development of a polder can be summarised as follows:

1. The enclosing dyke and pumping stations are built so that the land can be drained.
2. Reed seeds are sown over the exposed mud surface to promote soil drainage, prevent the invasion of weeds and to begin the soil ripening process.
3. The system of canals and drainage ditches as well as roads is constructed.
4. The reed vegetation is cleared and the soil prepared for the first crop – often oilrape.

5. The land is farmed for about five years as a large government agricultural estate.
6. During the period of temporary farming by the government, open ditches are replaced by subsurface drains and soils are improved. Farm buildings as well as all forms of services and other settlements are provided.
7. Farms are allocated to private individuals as family units; in the first Zuider Zee polder the smallest farms are c. 10 ha, but in the more recent polders the farms are as large as c. 70 ha.
8. Concurrent with farm allocation, progress is made in terms of rural landscaping, afforestation and the construction of recreational areas.
9. The final step involves the handing over of general administration from government bodies to local polder boards.

(After Smits, n.d. pp. 7–9)

One of the tasks of the Lake Yssel Development Authority is to carry out soil surveys of the Zuider Zee polders. Such surveys are first carried out from boats before drainage is complete! Within the former Zuider Zee there are marked variations in marine sediments; although these are all calcareous, they vary from clays to sands and peats. It is obviously desirable to choose areas of good soil potential for polders. Another vital early prediction from reconnaissance of 'soils' from boats is the likely amount of soil subsidence following drainage which depends on the amount and depth of clay. Sandy soils are not usually subject to subsidence whilst clay soils may settle by more than 1 m during the first 100 years (Edelman, 1963). Clearly, such differential subsidence could play havoc with drainage systems if account was not taken of these changes. As soon as conditions permit, the principal canals are excavated and such an operation generates a large quantity of marine sediment. The type of material likely to be encountered can be predicted from the reconnaissance survey and plans can be made so that excavated sands are reserved for constructional purposes, and clays are kept for mixing to improve sandy soils. Soon after a polder is pumped dry, a general soil survey is carried out. The results from such a survey aid the planning of the various reclamation processes such as canal excavation, spacing of temporary ditches, land division and required rates of fertilizer application. Finally, the soils of a new polder are surveyed in detail and the resultant information is used for a range of purposes which are summarised by Edelman (1963). A permanent system of soil drainage has to be designed and obviously soil conditions must be carefully considered. At the other extreme a water supply needs to be installed to fields which have soils susceptible to drought.

Farm size, layout, rent and general farming system have to be decided, and again the results of a detailed soil survey are helpful. When farms become fully operational, these results can aid farmers in their choice of tillage techniques, choice of crops and fertilizer requirements. The theme which clearly emerges in outlining the creation of the Zuider Zee polders is the integral role which soil survey plays within the overall and evolving planning process. A similar function of soil survey is apparent when consideration is given to the planning in the Netherlands of rural development and reconstruction.

The Netherlands, like many countries in western and southern Europe, has an inheritance of small farms with fields on individual farms often distributed in a fragmented manner. Such inefficient farm structures may also be further disadvantaged by the low standard of farm buildings and equipment, lack of good roads and the poor control of soil drainage. The need for land consolidation schemes has long been apparent and the first Land Consolidation Act was passed in 1924. The Government

Service for Land and Water Use was established in 1935 and is specifically responsible for the design, execution and supervision of land consolidation projects. The original Act was amended in 1938 and 1954 and the scheme is described by Herweijer (1964). Provision is made for land consolidation by two schemes. Consolidation of holdings within an area can take place if landowners voluntarily undertake to reorganise their holdings according to an agreed plan. Alternatively, such reconstruction is achieved by a statutory procedure in which the initiative usually comes from the government agency, though the ultimate plan has to be voted upon and approved by the landowners concerned before implementation is possible. This latter procedure is the more common one in the Netherlands. It needs to be stressed that a land consolidation project involves the total reorganisation of agrarian districts. Besides the consolidation of holdings and often the construction of new farms, new and improved roads, mains water and electricity are provided, water management is improved, provision is made for outdoor recreational facilities, and consideration is also given to nature conservancy and the preservation of landscape features of cultural interest. An example of this type of rural reorganisation for a river-clay area is given by Van den Ban (1964). In addition to the detailed planning processes necessary for land consolidation projects, there is also an array of financial schemes; for example farmers who are displaced from their land and retire early require to be financially compensated and farmers starting up on reorganised farms need help with capital in the initial years.

Detailed soil surveys aid in the planning of land consolidation projects. Haans and Westerveld (1970) report that 700 000 ha had been surveyed at scales of 1 : 10 000 or 1 : 25 000 by 1970 with about 60 000 ha being covered every year. The work has continued during the 1970s at a rate of 50 000 ha per year (Haans, 1978). The annual coverage of such a large area at a detailed scale requires that a significant number of surveyors in the Netherlands Soil Survey Institute are permanently employed on this applied work. Haans and Westerveld (1970) identify three types of maps which are useful in the rural planning process, viz.: (1) inventory maps (general soil maps, cross-sections); (2) derivative maps (maps showing the spatial distribution of selected attributes such as water-table classes, thickness and depth of peat); and (3) interpretative maps (for example, suitability assessments for a range of specific land uses, guidance on soil drainage or improvement needs). Such maps help with the layout of farms, the improvement of soil conditions and water control and the building of new roads (Edelman, 1963). It is interesting to consider briefly how soil information can be used in the design of reorganised farms.

In the consolidation process, farmers clearly have to give up certain fields and take over others. In no way would a farmer wish to give up fields with good soils in return for fields of poor soil, and thus the soil survey plays a key role in ensuring the equitable reallocation of fields. New fields are established and often new buildings, and again soil conditions are relevant to the planning operation. Figure 5.8 is an example of a derivative map showing the depth to a sand subsoil. It is best in terms of foundation costs if buildings and roads can be positioned so that they occur where sand is nearest the surface, and Fig. 5.8 shows how this can be achieved by a slight modification to the plan. Field boundaries should also be selected so that no major difference in soils occur within fields.

The reasons why the Netherlands was chosen as a case study to demonstrate the application of soil survey should now be abundantly clear. Soil information is used in the planning of a wide variety of land uses, from horticulture, agriculture, forestry and recreation, to urban areas. The integral nature of soil surveys in land reclamation and

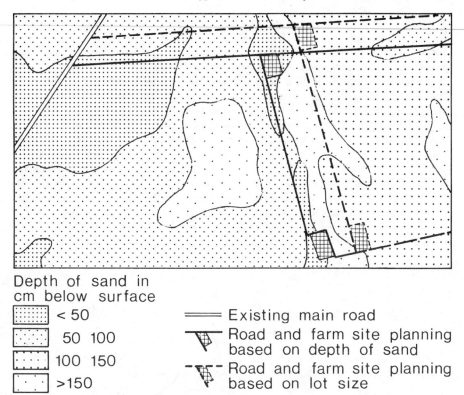

Depth of sand in cm below surface

▦ < 50	═══ Existing main road
▦ 50 100	⊽ Road and farm site planning based on depth of sand
▦ 100 150	-⊽- Road and farm site planning based on lot size
▦ >150	

Fig. 5.8   The map shows variation in depth to a sand subsoil, information which has been derived from a soil map. It is desirable that farm buildings and roads are built on areas where this sand is nearest to the surface (From Haans and Westerveld, 1970, p. 302).

consolidation schemes also needs to be stressed. The staff of the Soil Survey Institute provide expertise, not as external consultants but as members involved with the planning process. Such an approach is in marked contrast to the situation in many other countries. In Britain, for example, the apparently small impact of soil conditions on land use planning may well be due to the fact that soil surveyors are not sufficiently involved in planning.

However, it should not be inferred that the approach of soil survey in the Netherlands is directly relevant to other countries. In a sense evaluation of the Dutch physical environment is less complicated than in other countries because variations in climate, slope and elevation are small. Also, little consideration is given to processes and hazards as in most land capability schemes, a point brought out by Gibbons and Haans (1976) who compare the approaches to land appraisal in the Netherlands and Victoria, Australia. The Dutch methods of assessing soils for planning are strongly influenced by the nature of Dutch soils, as well as by the particular land use planning needs. By way of conclusion, it is instructive to consider some of the reasons which have resulted in such an applied soil survey tradition. The country is small and densely populated, averaging about 400 people per square kilometre. Such a density necessarily places great pressure on space and thus every effort is made to make optimum use of land. The country has a strong economy and can afford to support a well-staffed Soil Survey Institute. The traditional emphasis on horticulture and intensive agriculture also encouraged an applied soil survey tradition. The Dutch landscape is very much man-made and man-controlled. The importance of maintaining drainage ditches and canals as well as protecting the coastal sand dune belt is stressed in schools. The merit of this environmental education is the general awareness of the need for careful environmental management. Thus there tends to be fairly broad support for research concerned with the physical basis of the country. Legislation such as the Land Consolidation Act necessitates the detailed study of rural areas which are to be reorganised and thus soil surveys are required. The Netherlands Soil Survey Institute has also been active in publicising the application of its research; in fact, Figs 5.4a, b, c, d, e and f are extracts from such publicity material. The strength of applied soil survey can also be related to the efforts of individual soil scientists. Much credit must be given to Professor C. H. Edelman for encouraging such work, research which has been continued by the scientists whose work has been referred to in this chapter. In conclusion, then, a number of factors have combined to result in the strong tradition of soil survey research in the Netherlands being applied to land use planning.

CHAPTER 6
CONCLUSION

In the first chapter of this book, the need for careful evaluation of soils in relation to land use was stressed, and the following chapters concentrated on describing and exemplifying appropriate techniques. The wide range of methods and the many examples selected indicate the magnitude of research done on this topic. In terms of major advances in recent years, the FAO *Framework for land evaluation* (1976), the development of computer-based soil information systems, the distinct broadening of application of soil data to non-agricultural land uses, and the integration of soil information not only with other environmental data but also with economic analysis, can be identified as recurring research themes. In addition, advances in national soil surveys through the use of aerial photographs and the gradual development of automated methods of mapping and soil analysis mean that countries are developing large soil data banks, though there is great variation from country to country. At the international level, the FAO–Unesco *Soil map of the World* is a major achievement since it is the first global soil map based on information from all the national soil survey organisations. Thus there is available not only a growing body of soil information to aid land use planning, but also a wide spectrum of interpretation and evaluation techniques.

However, such optimistic remarks must be tempered with some caution. In many countries, very few, if any detailed soil maps are published. The absence, or virtual absence, of soil survey research necessarily creates serious difficulties for land use planning which ought to benefit from the availability of soil information. However, even in countries with well-established soil surveys, there are marked differences in the extent to which soil data are used in land use planning. The example of the Netherlands was selected to indicate the high level of involvement of soil scientists with planning, but as was suggested at the end of Chapter 5, there are some particular reasons why the situation is so favourable in that country. In the Netherlands, legislation such as the Land Consolidation Act ensures the active participation of soil scientists in planning. Progress is also evident in the USA and Canada in terms of legislation designed to conserve prime agricultural areas which can only be identified after detailed soil survey work. In Britain, despite the publication of many soil survey maps, soil scientists are not widely involved with land use planning. Instead, soil maps are primarily used in agricultural advisory work, though there is some evidence of an increasing demand for soil data for other purposes. One recurring problem associated with the interpretation of soil survey information for land use planning is that there is often a lack of knowledge about optimum soil requirements for specific land uses.

The aim of this book has been to demonstrate the applicability and particular advantages of utilising soil information for the planning of a wide range of land uses. The obvious inference is that there is much scope for the greater use of such information in land use planning. The necessary scientific expertise is available in many countries or can be obtained through international agencies or specialist survey companies, but the basic underlying problem is the frequent lack of awareness on the part of decision-makers about the availability and usefulness of soil data. In part this difficulty could be resolved by active publicity work such as that of the Netherlands Soil Survey Institute, but it is more common for soil surveys to be unwilling to try to sell their products in any extensive manner. Their view is often that their remit is to publish soil maps, and other organisations can then make use of the information as appropriate. This leads on to the point that soil survey institutes should not only advertise their maps more widely, but also encourage their members to become more involved with land use planning. This would depend upon a more liberal view of the function of a national soil survey. Also, of course, planning legislation ought to require the more active involvement of soil and other environmental scientists through insisting upon the careful evaluation of land resources prior to specific land use changes.

Land use planning decisions are usually made by planning committees elected on a local or regional basis. It is clearly important that committee members are aware of possible inputs of soil information to aid planning decisions. Again, this raises the need for soil surveys to publicise the type of work they undertake. In Britain, the training of planners often has an economic and sociological emphasis which means that the potential usefulness of soil information is not recognised. Thus there is the need not only for publicising the work of soil surveys to the general public, but also for planners to have some basic training in environmental subjects including soil science.

To conclude this short book, it is appropriate to consider how the application of soil information to land use planning can be improved. Clearly, there is still much scope for the development and refinement of soil survey techniques as well as subsequent evaluation procedures. There is need for the testing of such methods in a wide variety of environmental and economic situations. Governments must appreciate the clear advantages in terms of resource conservation and land development costs of giving strong support to soil survey institutes. In other words, such institutes need to be well staffed so that members can devote considerable time to specific land use planning issues. In turn this will require the training of more staff, preferably on a broader basis than has traditionally been the case in soil science.

Perhaps the greatest need is for a more widespread recognition of environmental issues in planning. In the public eye, such issues tend to be dominated by such themes as pollution, nature conservation, environmental hazards or erosion. Little attention is given to soil questions in Britain since the attitude is that any problems can easily be solved by appropriate fertilizer, drainage or engineering strategies. There is certainly a need for a more widespread appreciation of soil properties and of how soils can vary markedly over short distances. Thus one of the most important functions of geography, like other environmental subjects, is its educational role. Geography, whether taught at primary school or post-graduate level, ought to give students a clear impression of how we are dependent upon the careful management and utilisation of our basic physical resources. The quotation of Ćirić given at the beginning of Chapter 1 may seem rather optimistic. An increasing popular awareness of environmental qualities can be discerned, though there is much scope for a broader understanding of the basic issues. The evidence from various countries does suggest that increasing environmental awareness results in political activity designed to ensure the better utilisation of soil data for land use planning purposes. In essence then, the need in soils and land use planning is the spread of the word rather than the writing of a gospel.

APPENDIX 1
GLOSSARY OF SOIL SCIENCE TERMS

(Note that this is not a full list since only terms used in the text are included.)

argillic horizon: An illuvial horizon characterised by an accumulation of clays.

Atterberg limits: A soil can exist in a liquid, plastic or solid state, depending upon its moisture content. Atterberg limits refer to the boundary values of these states (see **liquid** and **plastic limit**).

base saturation: The extent to which exchange sites in a soil are saturated with exchangeable cations other than hydrogen and aluminium.

caliche: A near-surface layer cemented by secondary calcium or magnesium carbonate.

cation exchange: The exchange between cations in solution and cations held on the surfaces of soil colloids (clays and organic matter).

cation exchange capacity: The total amount of exchangeable cations that a soil can absorb expressed in milliequivalents per 100 g of soil (meq/100 g).

coat, soil: The lining or coating of a natural interface with such soil constituents as clays, sesquioxides or coarser material (through the removal of finer material).

colour, soil: The colour of soil horizons is described by using a Munsell Soil Colour Chart. Information is collected not only about dominant and subdominant colours in horizons but also about the moisture status, since this influences colour.

concretion, soil: See **nodule**.

consistence, soil: This property results from the kind of cohesion and adhesion. It is described according to strength (resistance of soil to crushing), type of failure, cementation, maximum stickiness and maximum plasticity (see **plasticity**).

dispersal index: The ratio between the total amount of very fine particles obtained by chemical and mechanical dispersion and the amount of the same material obtained by mechanical dispersion.

electrical conductivity, soil: Measured to indicate the salt concentration in soil. Measures are made in units of milli-reciprocal ohms per centimetre (mmhos/cm). Values less than 4 mmhos/cm (approximately equivalent to less than 3 000 ppm salts in solution) suggest that most crops should not suffer from salinity conditions.

erodibility: The resistance of soil particles to detachment and transportation. It depends upon soil properties such as texture, aggregate stability, and organic content as well as upon topographic position and slope value.

fragment, soil: A soil aggregate, like a clod, less permanent than a ped. Fragments occur at or near the surface and result from cultivation or frost action.

gilgai: Microrelief of soils produced by expansion and contraction resultant upon moisture changes. Gilgai is associated with expansive clays.

gleyed soil: A soil developed under poor drainage conditions, indicated by the reduction of iron and other elements, grey colours and mottles.

horizon, soil: A layer of soil approximately parallel to the soil surface. It differs from adjacent layers in terms of colour, and often also structure, texture, consistence, and chemical, biological and mineralogical composition.

horizon boundary: A description of the boundary between soil horizons. Such terms as sharp, clear, gradual or diffuse are used to indicate the clarity of the boundary whilst the form of the boundary is also described by such terms as smooth, wavy, irregular or broken.

horizon notation: Horizons are designated by the use of letters to permit the comparison and classification of profiles. Examples are L for a fresh litter horizon, F a partly decomposed litter horizon, H a well-decomposed organic layer, A an upper mineral horizon which also includes organic matter, E (or A₂) a subsurface horizon which is lighter is colour and contains less organic matter, iron, aluminium or clay than the immediately underlying horizon, B a subsurface mineral horizon with the illuvial concentration of clay, iron, aluminium or humus, and C the parent material from which the soil has developed.

hydraulic conductivity: The rate at which water can move through soil. One experimental technique for determining its value is to drill a hole to below the water table. The water is then pumped out of the hole, and from measurements of the rate of rise of water, the value of hydraulic conductivity can be calculated.

infiltration rate: The maximum rate at which water can enter a soil under specified conditions.

leaching: The transfer of material within the soil by solution.

liquid limit: The moisture content at which a soil changes from a plastic to a liquid state.

mottle: A spot of colour or shade interspersed with, and different from, the dominant colour of a soil horizon. Mottles are distinct from colour variation associated with ped surfaces, worm holes, concretions or nodules.

nodule, soil: A unit within soil, different from the surrounding material because of the concentration of some constituent (for example calcium carbonate). Usually nodules are cemented and hard. Concretions are nodules which are more symmetrical owing to a more concentric accumulation process.

numerical taxonomy: The use of statistical techniques in order to classify soils.

particle size class: Size ranges of particle size are labelled by such terms as clay, fine silt, medium silt, coarse silt, fine sand, medium sand and coarse sand.

ped: Relatively permanent soil aggregate, separated by voids or natural surfaces of weakness.

pedalfer: A soil in which iron and aluminium sesquioxides increase relative to silica during soil development. An example is a podzol.

pedocal: A soil in which calcium carbonate accumulates during soil development. An example is a chernozem.

pedon: The smallest three-dimensional unit of soil which can be examined.

pH, soil: A measure of the hydrogen ion concentration in soils. Values below 7 indicate acid conditions whilst values above 7 indicate alkalinity.

phase, soil: A subdivision of a soil series according to variations in such properties as depth of horizons or stoniness.

plasticity: The ability of soil to change shape constantly when stress is applied and to retain the new shape after the stress is removed.

plasticity index: The difference between the plastic and liquid limits.

plastic limit: The moisture content at which a soil changes from a solid to a plastic state.

salinity: See **electrical conductivity**.

series, soil: A grouping of soil profiles to permit the mapping of soils. Each series, named after a locality where it is well represented, is characterised by a similar sequence of horizons developed on uniform parent materials and under similar drainage conditions.

sierozem: (obsolete term). A soil type found in arid and semi-arid areas and characterised by a low organic content, a lack of leaching and an accumulation of calcium carbonate in middle and lower horizons.

solod: A soil which develops from the leaching of a solonetz with the formation of a bleached E horizon which, as in a podzol, is deficient in iron and aluminium, has a sandy texture and is acid. The underlying B horizon is gleyed and has a columnar structure developed in clays.

solonchak: A light-coloured soil with a high concentration of soluble salts (sodium chloride and sodium sulphate).

solonetz: A dark-coloured soil which develops from a solonchak by leaching of some of the sodium which has the effect of deflocculating the soil mass. The soil develops a characteristic columnar structure when dry and is highly alkaline.

structure, soil: The shape, size and degree of development of the aggregation of primary soil particles into naturally or artificially formed structural units called peds, clods or fragments (see **fragment**). Terms such as 'platy', 'prismatic', 'blocky', 'crumb' and 'granular' are used to describe the shape of peds and fragments.

texture, soil: The relative proportions of sand, silt and clay defining soil textural classes such as sandy clay, clay loam, sandy clay loam, silty clay loam, etc.

Unified Soil Classification System: A classification based on certain engineering properties of soils, viz. optimum moisture content, permeability, compressibility and shear strength.

void: A space in soil not occupied by solid matter. This space can be occupied by soil water, or the soil atmosphere.

void ratio: A ratio of the volume of void space to the volume of solid matter in a soil mass.

warp soil: A soil developed from alluvial or estuarine deposits, artificially raised by controlled sedimentation above the level of normal alluvial soils. Warp soils are usually 50–75 cm thick and frequently show the original laminae laid down in the process of accumulation. These soils are often neutral or slightly alkaline in reaction.

APPENDIX 2
LAND JUDGING FORM

(From Burnham and McRae, 1974, pp. 109–11)

Locality .... Observer ....

Soil series .... Date ....

		Best possible class
Climate (subclass c)		
A Elevation (in metres)		
< 150	1	
150–230	2	
230–380	3	
380–450	4	
450–530	5	
530–610	6	
> 610	7	_____ c
B Mean rainfall (mm/annum)		
< 1 010 mm	1	
1 010–1 140	2	
1 140–1 270	3	
1 270–1 520		
(a) if less than 150 m	4	
(b) if higher than 150 m	5	
> 1 520 mm		
(a) if less than 300 m	5	
(b) if higher than 300 m	6	_____ c
C Mean daily maximum temperature April/September		
> 15°	1	
14–15°	3	
< 14°	4	_____ c

D   Exposure to wind

Sheltered or moderately exposed	1	
Very exposed	2	c

Gradient (subclass g)

E   Angle of slope

< 7°	1	
7–11°	3	
11–15°	4	
15–25°	5	
> 25°	6	g

Erosion (subclass e)

F   Liability to water erosion (including evidence of past erosion)

Negligible to slight	1	
Moderate	2	
Severe	5	e

G   Liability to wind erosion

Negligible to slight	1	
Moderate to severe	2	
Shifting sand dunes	7	e

Soil limitations (subclass s)

H   Boulders (> 20 cm in diameter) or rock outcrops

None	1	
Few	4	
Many	6	
Dominant	7	s

J   Stoniness

Stoneless or slightly stony	1	
Stoniness a nuisance	2	
Stoniness precludes ploughing	5	s

K   Rootable depth (cm)
(i.e. depth of soil above a physical barrier to root growth, e.g. bedrock)

> 75 cm	1	
50–75 cm	2	
25–50 cm	3	
15–25 cm	4	
< 15 cm	6	s

L   Texture of uppermost 20 cm

Fine sand, sandy loam, silt loam, silt or peat with some mineral mixture	1	

Coarse sand or loamy coarse sand:
  (*a*) if summer moisure deficit occurs 6 years or less in 10   1
  (*b*) if summer moisture deficit occurs 7 years or more in 10   3
Clay loam or clay   2
Peat without mineral mixture   2   _____ s

M Evidence of bleached podzol horizon
No   1
Yes, but soil mottled within 90 cm or surface   2
Yes, but no such mottling   3   _____ s

Wetness (subclass w)

N Liability to damaging flood (years in 10)
0   1
1   2
2   4
> 2   5   _____ w

P Springs or permanently waterlogged patches
None   1
Few   2
Many   5   _____ w

Q Water regime (topsoil)
Annual period of waterlogging in top 30 cm
< 1 month   1
1–2 months
  if rainfall < 760 mm   1
  if rainfall > 760 mm   2
3–6 months   3
> 6 months   5   _____ w

R Water regime (subsoil)
Annual period of waterlogging in 30–60 cm zone
< 1 month   1
1–6 months
  if rainfall < 760 mm   1
  if rainfall > 760 mm   2
> 6 months   3   _____ w

S Morphological evidence of gleying in topsoil (0–30 cm)
  (for use only if Q and R cannot be applied
No signs of gleying   1
Rusty root mottles   3   _____ w

T Morphological evidence of gleying in 30–60 cm zone
  (for use only if Q and R cannot be applied)
No signs of gleying   1
Ochreous mottles only below 45 cm   1

Ochreous mottles in 30–45 cm zone and distinct
  mottling in greys and brown below this
  (*a*) if rainfall < 760 mm   1
  (*b*) if rainfall > 760 mm   2
Prominent grey and ochreous mottles, streaks
  or root tubes at less than 45 cm   3   w

U Subsoil permeability

Unimpeded   1
Slow   2
Impermeable   3   w

V Feasibility of artificial drainage

Unnecessary or totally effective   1
Economically feasible but not totally
  effective   3
Economically marginal, but could enable arable
  cultivation   4
Limited improvement possible to maintain
  grassland   5
Necessary but technically or economically
  impracticable   6   w

	First approximation	**Final decision**
Land capability class		
Subclass		

Reasons for classification ....

APPENDIX 3
LEGEND OF THE GENERAL SOIL SUITABILITY MAP FOR ARABLE LAND AND GRASSLAND IN THE NETHERLANDS

(From Vink and van Zuilen, 1974, pp. 53–5)

MAJOR CLASS BG

Arable land and grassland soils

Soils generally suited to arable land and usually also to grassland.

BG1   Arable land and grassland soils of very wide suitability
generally, if well drained, very well suited to most arable crops, with good to very good yields and a high yield security, locally slightly drought-susceptible; with good water management well suited to grassland, but partly with a summer depression, very good fodder quality.

BG2   Arable land and grassland soils of wide suitability
generally, if well drained, well suited to most arable crops but with limitations for some crops and/or a lower yield security; generally well suited to grassland, but with a more or less strong summer depression, very good fodder quality.

    BG2a   with limitations caused by chemical and/or physical properties (clay content, structure, potash fixation, lime deficiency, luxuriancy).

    BG2b   with limitations caused by slope and/or age of the soils.

BG3   Arable land and grassland soils of fairly limited suitability
generally, with adequate water management, well suited and locally very well suited to a limited crop rotation with wheat as principal cereal crop, locally however less favourable or even unsuitable; moderately to well suited to grassland—the wetter parts late in spring—sometimes with a more or less strong summer depression, good to very good fodder quality.

BG4   Arable land and grassland soils of limited suitability
well to very well suited to an extensive rotation with rye as principal cereal crop, locally also to some commercial crops—the wetter parts, however, are too hazardous for winter crops; moderately to well and locally very well suited to grassland, good fodder quality.

BG5   Arable land and grassland soils of very limited suitability
generally well suited to rye, oats, potatoes and mangolds—the more loamy and/or clayey or humose parts are also more or less suited to sugar-beet and/or wheat; more or less suited to permanent grassland.

BG6   Arable land and grassland complex of strongly varying suitability
soils varying considerably over short distances: the best parts are equivalent to those of class BG2; considerable areas, however, poorly suited to arable land and grassland are also included.

BG7   Arable land and grassland complex of limited suitability
soils with a suitability varying considerably over short distances: the drier parts are
generally well suited to rye, oats and potatoes, locally also to mangolds and poorly suited to
grassland; the wetter parts are poorly suited to arable land but well suited to grassland with
a good gross production and a slight summer depression, well suited to grazing, moderate
to good fodder quality.

MAJOR CLASS GB

Grassland and arable land soils

Soils generally suited to grassland and in many cases also to arable land.

GB1   Grassland and arable land soils of fairly limited suitability
productive grassland soils—the driest parts with a slight summer depression, the wettest
late in spring, locally too wet for grassland, well suited to grazing, good fodder quality; the
well-drained loamy or clayey parts are well to very well suited to an extensive rotation with
rye as principal cereal crop, in some cases to a limited rotation with wheat as principal
cereal crop and locally also for some commercial crops, the other soils are partly too wet
and/or too heavy for arable land.

GB2   Grassland and arable land soils of limited suitability
grassland soils with a good gross production, but often late in spring, locally poorly suited to
grazing (too wet), moderate fodder quality; generally more or less suited to an extensive
rotation with rye as principal cereal crop, but partly too hazardous for winter crops—the
wetter parts are unsuitable for arable land.

GB3   Grassland and arable land complex of limited suitability
soils of strongly varying quality when under grass—the best parts have a good gross
production, are late in spring, but without summer depression, the driest parts have a low
gross production with a strong summer depression, the wettest parts are too wet for use as
grassland—moderate to good fodder quality; the soils have in some parts a limited
suitability, but are in general too heavy and/or too wet and/or too peaty for arable land.

MAJOR CLASS B

Arable land soils

Soils generally suited to arable land, but mostly poorly or not suited to grassland.

B1   Arable land soils of limited suitability
only suited to drought-resistant and/or early crops, locally well suited to a few commercial
crops; at most moderately suited to permanent grassland (low gross production).

B2   Arable land soils of very limited suitability
generally well suited to rye, oats and potatoes and in the wetter or more moisture-retaining
areas also to mangolds.

B3   Arable land soils of extremely limited suitability
generally at most moderately suited to rye, oats and potatoes.

MAJOR CLASS G

Grassland soils

Soils generally suited to grassland, but mostly poorly or not suited to arable land.

G1   Firm sensitive grassland soils
with a good gross production, but very sensitive to a good water management, sometimes late in spring, with a sufficiently firm sod, good fodder quality.

G2   Firm late grassland soils
with a good gross production, often late in spring, sometimes with a more or less strong summer depression, firm sod, moderate to good fodder quality.

G3   Soft sensitive grassland soils
with a good gross production, very sensitive to a good water management, usually late in spring, having a very sensitive sod under poor water management, strongly varying fodder quality.

G4   Grassland soils of varying suitability
generally with a good gross production—the driest parts with a summer depression, the wetter parts late in spring and sometimes with a soft sod—moderate to good fodder quality.

G5   Grassland soils of moderate suitability
generally with a moderate gross production—locally too wet or too dry—moderate fodder quality.

MAJOR CLASS O

Unsuitable soils

Soils predominantly poorly suited to arable land and to grassland.

O1   Predominantly too dry soils

O2   Predominantly too wet soils

NON-CLASSIFIED

I   Areas with extremely varying soils or hydrology and reclaimed sand excavations

II   Foreland soils

Urban areas

Water

REFERENCES

Agricultural Land Service (1966) *Agricultural land classification*, Ministry of Agriculture, Fisheries and Food, Technical Report No. 11.

Agricultural Development and Advisory Service (1976) *Agricultural land classification of England and Wales: the definition and identification of sub-grades within grade 3*, Ministry of Agriculture, Fisheries and Food, Technical Report 11/1, HMSO.

Albers, H. T. M. P., Krul, H. A. and **van Lanen, H. A. J.** (1975) *Some existing West European land classification systems compared with recent FAO standards*, Land Suitability Classification Report, Part 2, Department of Soil Science and Geology, Agricultural University, Wageningen, the Netherlands.

Arlidge, E. Z. (1973) *Land resouces and agricultural suitability, map of Mauritius 1 : 50 000*, FAO and Mauritius Sugar Industry Research Institute.

Arlidge, E. Z. and **Cheong, Y. W. Y.** (1975) 'Notes on the land resources and agricultural suitability map of Mauritius 1 : 50 000', Occasional Paper No. 29, Mauritius Sugar Industry Research Institute.

Armstrong, D. W. and **Wetherby, K. G.** (1977) 'Computer assistance in the preparation of a detailed soil survey of the Padthaway irrigation area', in Moore, A. W. and Bie, S. W. (eds), *Uses of soil information systems*, Centre for Agricultural Publishing and Documentation, Wageningen, the Netherlands, pp. 44–50.

Atlas van Nederland (1963–77) Staatsdrukkerij-en Uitgeverijbedrijf, 's-Gravenhage.

Avery, B. W. (1973) 'Soil classification in the soil survey of England and Wales', *Journal of Soil Science* **24**, 324–38.

Bartelli, L. J. (1962) 'Use of soils information in urban-fringe areas', *Journal of Soil and Water Conservation* **17**, 99–103.

Bartelli, L. J. *et al.* (eds) (1966) *Soil surveys and land use planning*, Soil Science Society of America and American Society of Agronomy, Madison, Wisconsin.

Bauer, K. W. (1973) 'The use of soils data in regional planning', *Geoderma* **10**, 1–26.

Bawden, M. G. and **Carroll, D. M.** (1968) *The land resources of Lesotho*, Land Resource Study No. 7, Land Resources Development Centre, Ministry of Overseas Development, Surbiton, England.

Bawden, M. G., Carroll, D. M. and **Tuley, P.** (1972) *The land resources of North East Nigeria. Volume 3, The land systems*, Land Resource Study No. 9, Land Resources Development Centre, Ministry of Overseas Development, Surbiton, England.

Beatty, M. T. and **Bouma, J.** (1973) 'Application of soil surveys to selection of sites for on-site disposal of liquid household wastes', *Geoderma* **10**, 113–22.

Beckett, P. H. T. (1978) 'The rate of soil survey in Britain', *Journal of Soil Science* **29**, 95–101.

Beckett, P. H. T., Webster, R., McNeil, G. M. and **Mitchell, C. W.** (1972) 'Terrain evaluation by means of a data bank', *Geographical Journal* **138**, 430–56.

Beek, K. J. (1975) 'Land utilization types in land evaluation' in *Land evaluation in Europe*, FAO Soils Bulletin No. 29, Rome, pp. 87–106.

Beek, K. J. (1977) 'The selection of soil properties and land qualities relevant to specific land uses in developing countries', in *Soil resources inventories*, Agronomy Mimeo No. 77–23, Cornell University, Ithaca, New York, pp. 143–62.

Beek, K. J. (1978) *Land evaluation for agricultural development*, Publication No. 23, International Institute for Land Reclamation and Improvement, Wageningen, the Netherlands.

Beek, K. J. and **Bennema, J.** (1972) *Land evaluation for agricultural land use planning: an ecological methodology*, Department of Soil Science and Geology, Agricultural University, Wageningen, the Netherlands.

Bentley, C. F. (1978) 'Canada's agricultural land resources and the world food problem', *Plenary Session Papers, 11th International Congress of Soil Science, Edmonton*, Vol. 2, 1–26

Bergmann, H. and **Boussard, J.** (1976) *Guide to the economic evaluation of irrigation projects*, OECD, Paris.

Best, R. H. (1973) 'Land conversions to urban use', *SSRC Newsletter* **19**, 11–13.

Best, R. H. (1976) 'The changing land use structure of Britain', *Town and County Planning* **44**, 171–6.

Bibby, J. S. and **Mackney, D.** (1969) *Land use capability classification*, Technical Monograph No. 1, Soil Survey, Harpenden.

Bie, S. W. (ed.) (1975) *Soil information systems*, Centre for Agricultural Publishing and Documentation, Wageningen, the Netherlands.

Bie, S. W. *et al.* (1976) 'Computer-aided interactive soil suitability classification – a simple Bayesian approach', *Netherlands Journal of Agricultural Science* **24**, 179–86.

Birkeland, P. W. (1974) *Pedology, weathering, and geomorphological research*, Oxford University Press, New York.

Birse, E. L. and **Dry, T. F.** (1970) *Assessment of climatic conditions in Scotland. 1. Based on accumulated temperature and potential water deficit*, Soil Survey of Scotland, Aberdeen.

Birse, E. L. and **Robertson, L.** (1970) *Assessment of climatic conditions in Scotland. 2. Based on exposure and accumulated frost*, Soil Survey of Scotland, Aberdeen.

Bowser, W. E. and **Moss, H. C.** (1950) 'A soil rating and classification for irrigation lands in western Canada', *Scientific Agriculture* **30**, 165–71.

Brady, N. C. (1974) *The nature and properties of soils*, 8th edn, Macmillan, New York.

Bridges, E. M. (1978) 'Soil geography, its content and literature', *Journal of Geography in Higher Education* **1**, 61–72.

Bridges, E. M. (1980) *World soils*, 2nd edn, Cambridge University Press, Cambridge.

Briggs, D. (1977) *Soils*, Butterworths, London.

Brinkman, R. and **Smyth, A. J.** (eds) (1973) *Land evaluation for rural purposes*, Publication No. 17, International Institute for Land Reclamation and Improvement, Wageningen, the Netherlands.

Brook, R. H. (1975) *Soil survey interpretation: an annotated bibliography*, Bibliography No. 10, International Institute for Land Reclamation and Improvement, Wageningen, the Netherlands.

Brunsden, D. *et al.* (1975) 'Large scale geomorphological mapping and highway engineering design', *Quarterly Journal of Engineering Geology* **8**, 227–53.

Bunting, B. T. (1972) *The geography of soil*, Hutchinson, London.

Bureau of Reclamation (1953) *Land classification handbook*, United States Department of the Interior, Bureau of Reclamation Publication V, Part 2, Washington DC.

Burnham, C. P. and **McRae, S. G.** (1974) 'Land judging', *Area* **6**, 107–11.

Canada Soil Survey Committee (1978) *The system of soil classification for Canada*, Canada Department of Agriculture, rev. edns in 1974 and 1978.

Carroll, D. M., Evans, R. and **Bendelow, V. C.** (1977) *Air photo-interpretation for soil mapping*, Technical Monograph No. 8, Soil Survey, Harpenden.

Centre for Agricultural Strategy (1976) *Land for agriculture*, Report 1, University of Reading, England.

Christian, C. S. and **Stewart, G. A.** (1952) *Summary of general report on survey of Katherine–Darwin Region, 1946*, CSIRO Land Research Series 1.

Christian, C. S. and **Stewart, G. A.** (1968) 'Methodology of integrated surveys', in *Aerial surveys and integrated studies*, Unesco, Paris, pp. 233–80.

Ćirić, M. (1975) Foreword to S. W. Bie (ed.), *Soil information systems*, Proceedings of the meeting of the ISS Working Group on Soil Information Systems, Centre for Agricultural Publishing and Documentation, Wageningen, the Netherlands, pp. 1–3.

Clarke, G. R. (1951) 'The evaluation of soils and the definition of quality classes from studies of the physical properties of the soil profile in the field', *Journal of Soil Science* **2**, 50–60.

Clarke, G. R. (1971) *The study of the soil in the field*, 5th edn, Clarendon Press, Oxford.

Clawson, M. (1972) *America's land and its uses*, Johns Hopkins Press, Baltimore.

Coen, G. M. and **Holland, W. D.** (1976) *Soils of Waterton Lakes National Park, Alberta*, Alberta Institute of Pedology Report S-73-33.

Coen, G. M., Epp, P. F., Tajek, J. and **Knapik, L.** (1977) *Soil survey of Yoho National Park, Canada*, Alberta Soil Survey Report No. 37 and Alberta Institute of Pedology Report No. S-77-37.

Coleman, D. J. (1975) *An ecological input to regional planning*, School of Urban and Regional Planning, University of Waterloo, Canada.

Collins, R. C. (1976) 'Agricultural land preservation in a land use planning perspective', *Journal of Soil and Water Conservation* **31,** 182–9.

Cooke, R. U. and **Doornkamp, J. C.** (1974) *Geomorphology in environmental management*, Oxford University Press, London.

Corcoran, P., Jarvis, M. G., Mackney, D. and **Stevens, K. W.** (1977) 'Soil corrosiveness in south Oxfordshire', *Journal of Soil Science* **28,** 473–84.

Countryside Commission for Scotland (1971) 'A planning classification of Scottish landscape resources', Countryside Commission for Scotland, Occasional Paper No. 1.

Courtney, F. M. and **Trudgill, S. T.** (1976) *The soil: an introduction to soil study in Britain*, Edward Arnold, London

Cratchley, C. R. and **Denness, B.** (1972) 'Engineering geology in urban planning with an example from the new city of Milton Keynes', *Proceedings 24th International Geological Congress, Montreal*, Section 13, 13–22.

Cruickshank, J. G. (1972) *Soil geography*, David and Charles, Newton Abbot.

Cruickshank, J. G. and **Armstrong, W. J.** (1971) 'Soil and agricultural land classification in County Londonderry', *Transactions of the Institute of British Geographers* **53,** 79–94.

Culver, V. P. and **Clonts, H. A.** (1976) *Alabama's land resources: a review of the need for critical areas protection*, Bulletin 481 Agricultural Experiment Station, Auburn University, Auburn, Alabama.

Curtis, L. F., Courtney, F. M. and **Trudgill, S.** (1976) *Soils in the British Isles*, Longman, London.

Davidson, D. A. (ed.) (1976a) *Soil survey interpretation and use*, Report No. 17, Welsh Soils Discussion Group.

Davidson, D. A. (1976b) 'Terrain evaluation: testing a technique in lower Deeside', *Scottish Geographical Magazine* **92,** 108–19.

Davidson, D. A. (1976c) 'Processes of tell formation and erosion', in Davidson, D. A. and Shackley, M. L. (eds) *Geoarchaeology: earth science and the past*, Duckworth, London, pp. 255–65.

de Bakker, G. (1950) (Soil conditions of some Zuid-Beveland polders and their adaptation for fruit growing) *Verslagen van Landbouwkundige Onderzoekingen*, No. 56.14.

de Bakker, H. (1979)*Major soils and soil regions in the Netherlands*, Centre for Agricultural Publishing and Documentation, Wageningen, the Netherlands.

de Bakker, H. and **Schelling, J.** (1966) *(System of soil classification for the Netherlands: the higher orders)*, Centre for Agricultural Publications and Documentation, Wageningen, the Netherlands.

Dekkers, J. M. T., Zegers, H. J. M., and **Westerveld, G. J. W.** (1972) *Deel van de bodemkartering ten behoeve van het structuurplan Helmond e.o. (gebied Brouwhuis)*, Stichting voor Bodemkartering, Wageningen.

Department of Regional and Economic Expansion (1970) *The Canada Land Inventory: objectives, scope and organization*, Report No. 1, 2nd edn, Ottawa.

Dudal, R. (1978) 'Land resources for agricultural development', *Plenary Session Papers, 11th International Congress of Soil Science, Edmonton*, Vol. 2, 314–40.

Dumanski, J., Kloosterman, B. and **Brandon, S. E.** (1975) 'Philosophy, structure and objectives of the Canada soil information system', *Canadian Journal of Soil Science* **55,** 181–7.

Edelman, C. H. (1963) *Applications of soil survey in land development in Europe*, International Institute for Land Reclamation and Improvement Publication No. 12, Wageningen, the Netherlands.

Eswaran, H., Forbes, T. R. and **Laker, M. C.** (1977) 'Soil map parameters and classification', in *Soil resource inventories*, Agronomy Mimeo No. 77–23, Cornell University, Ithaca, New York, pp. 37–57.

FAO (1974a) *FAO–UNESCO, Soil map of the world*, Vol. 1, *Legend*, Unesco, Paris.

FAO (1974b) *Approaches to land classification*, Soils Bulletin No. 22, FAO, Rome.

FAO (1975) *Land evaluation in Europe*, FAO Soils Bulletin No. 29, Rome.

FAO (1976) *A framework for land evaluation*, FAO Soils Bulletin No. 32, Rome.

Fenton, T. E. (1975) 'Use of soil productivity ratings in evaluating Iowa agricultural land', *Journal of Soil and Water Conservation* **30,** 237–40.

Fenton, T. E., Duncan, E. R., Shrader, W. D. and **Dumenil, L. C.** (1971) *Productivity levels of some Iowa soils*, Agriculture and Home Economics Experiment Station, Special Report No. 66, Iowa State University of Science and Technology, Ames, Iowa.

FitzPatrick, E. A. (1971) *Pedology*, Oliver and Boyd, Edinburgh.

FitzPatrick, E. A. (1974) *An introduction to soil science*, Oliver and Boyd, Edinburgh.

Foth, H. D. and **Turk, L. M.** (1972) *Fundamentals of soil science*, 5th edn, Wiley, New York.

Garbouchev, I. P. and **Sadovski, A. N.** (1978) 'Development and use of soil information systems in Europe', *Symposia Papers, 11th International Congress of Soil Science, Edmonton*, Vol. 3, pp. 132–42.

Gibbons, F. R. and **Haans, J. C. F. M.** (1976) *Dutch and Victorian approaches to land appraisal*, Soil Survey Papers No. 11, Netherlands Soil Survey Institute, Wageningen, the Netherlands.

Gilg, A. W. (1975) 'Development control and agricultural land quality', *Town and Country Planning* **43**, 387–9.

Gillespie, J. E., Wicklund, R. E. and **Miller, M. H.** (n.d.) *The soils of Halton County*, Report No. 43, Ontario Soil Survey, Ontario Department of Agriculture and Food, Toronto.

Government of Ontario (1977) *Planning for agriculture: food land guidelines* (Green Paper).

Griffiths, E. (1975) *Classification of land for irrigation in New Zealand*, New Zealand Soil Bureau Scientific Report No. 22, Department of Scientific and Industrial Research, New Zealand.

Grigg, D. (1970) *The harsh lands: a study in agricultural development*, Macmillan, London.

Haans, J. C. F. M. (1975) 'Soil survey interpretation in the Netherlands', paper presented at the Technical Consultation on Land Evaluation for Europe, Nitra, Czechoslovakia.

Haans, J. C. F. M. (1978) 'Soil survey interpretations in the Netherlands', paper presented at a symposium between The Netherlands and Rumania, September, 1978.

Haans, J. C. F. M. and **van Lynden, K. R.** (1978) 'Assessment factors as an aid for interpreting soil surveys', paper presented at 11th International Congress of Soil Science, Edmonton, Canada.

Haans, J. C. F. M. and **Westerveld, G. J. W.** (1970) 'The application of soil survey in the Netherlands', *Geoderma* **4**, 279–309.

Haantjens, H. A. and **Bleeker, P.** (1975) 'Procedures for computer storage of soil and landscape data from Papua New Guinea. II. Input of soil capability and soil classification data', *Geoderma* **13**, 115–28.

Hagan, R. M., Haise, R. R. and **Edminster, T. W.** (eds) (1967) *Irrigation of agricultural lands*, American Society of Agronomy, Madison, Wisconsin.

Hannam, I. D., Emery, K. A. and **Murphy, B. W.** (1978) *Land resources study of the city of Bathurst*, Soil Conservation Service of New South Wales.

Hart, J. F. (1976) 'Urban encroachment on rural areas', *Geographical Review* **66**, 3–17.

Hartnup, R. (1976) 'Soil survey as a tool for planners', *Welsh Soils Discussion Group Report* No. 17, 135–47.

Hartnup, R. and **Jarvis, R. A.** (1973) *Soils of the Castleford area of Yorkshire*, Special Survey No. 8, Soil Survey of England and Wales, Harpenden.

Hazelden, J., Beckett, P. H. T. and **Jarvis, M. G.** (1976) 'A computer-compatible proforma for field soil records', *Geoderma* **15**, 21–9.

Herweijer, S. (1964) 'Natural and planned adjustment of the countryside', *Planning and Development in the Netherlands* **2**, 22–34.

Hewgill, D. (1977) 'Land capability classification for the Maltby sheet (SK59)', *Proceedings North of England Soil Discussion Group* **13**, 15–18.

Highlands and Islands Development Board (1971) *Comprehensive Development Report on Mull*, Inverness.

Hills, G. A. (1976) 'An integrated iterative holistic approach to ecosystem classification', in Thie, J. and Ironside, G. (eds), *Ecological (biophysical) land classification in Canada*, Ecological Land Classification Series No. 1, Lands Directorate, pp. 73–97.

Hockensmith, R. D. and **Steele, J. G.** (1949) 'Recent trends in the use of the land capability classification', *Proceedings of the Soil Science Society of America*, **14**, 383–8.

Hodgson, J. M. (1974) *Soil survey field handbook*, Technical Monograph No. 5, Soil Survey, Harpenden.

Hodgson, J. M. (1978) *Soil sampling and soil description*, Oxford University Press, Oxford.

Hudson, N. (1971) *Soil conservation*, Batsford, London.

Hudson, N. W. (1975) *Field engineering for agricultural development*, Oxford University Press, London.

International Institute for Land Reclamation and Improvement (1977) *A framework for land evaluation*, Publication No. 22, International Institute for Land Reclamation and Improvement, Wageningen, the Netherlands.

Jacks, G. V. (1946) *Land classification*, Imperial Bureau of Soil Science, Technical Communication No. 43.

Jacks, G. V. (1954) *Soil*, Nelson, London.

Jenkin, R. N. *et al.* (1976) *The agricultural development potential of the Belize Valley, Belize*, Land Resource Study No. 24, Land Resources Development Centre, Ministry of Overseas Development, Surbiton, England.

Joffe, J. S. (1949) *Pedology*, Pedology Publications, New Brunswick, New Jersey.

Junor, R. S., Emery, K. A. and **Crouch, R. J.** (1977) *Land resources study of the Albury–Wodonga growth centre in New South Wales*, Soil Conservation Service of New South Wales, Australia.

Keith, G. S. (1811) *A general view of the agriculture of Aberdeenshire*, Aberdeen.

Kellogg, C. E. (1951) 'Soil and land classification', *Journal of Farm Economics* **33**, 499–513.

Kellogg, C. E. and **Orvedal, A. C.** (1969) 'Potentially arable soils of the world and critical measures for their use' *Advances in Agronomy* **21**, 109–70.

King, R. B. (1970) 'A parametric approach to land system classification', *Geoderma* **4**, 37–46.

King, R. B. (1975) 'Geomorphic and soil correlation analysis of land systems in Northern and Luapula Provinces of Zambia', *Transactions of the Institute of British Geography* **64**, 67–76.

King, R. B. and **Birchall, C. J.** (1975) *Land systems and soils of the Southern Rift Valley, Ethiopia*, Land Resource Report No. 5, Land Resources Development Centre, Ministry of Overseas Development, Surbiton, England.

Klingebiel, A. A. (1966) 'Costs and returns of soil surveys', *Soil Conservation* **32**, 3–6.

Klingebiel, A. A. and **Montgomery, P. H.** (1961) *Land capability classification*, United States Department of Agriculture Handbook No. 210.

Knebel, J. A. (1976) 'Statement on prime farmland, range, and forest land', US Department of Agriculture, Secretary's Memorandum No. 1827, Supplement 1, also reproduced in *Journal of Soil and Water Conservation* **31**, 184–5.

Lapping, M. B. (1975) 'Preserving agricultural lands: the New York experience', *Town and Country Planning* **43**, 394–7.

Lawrance, C. J. (1972) *Terrain evaluation in West Malaysia: Part 1, Terrain classification and survey methods*, Transport and Road Research Laboratory Report LR 506.

Lawrance, C. J. (1978) *Terrain evaluation in West Malaysia: Part 2, land systems of South West Malaysia*, Transport and Road Research Laboratory Supplementary Report No. 378.

Lawrance, C. J. *et al.* (1977) 'The use of air photo interpretation for land evaluation in the western highlands of Scotland', *Catena* **4**, 341–57.

Leamy, M. L. (1974a) 'Resources of highly productive land', *New Zealand Agricultural Science* **8**, 187–91.

Leamy, M. L. (1974b) *An improved method of assessing the soil factor in land valuation*, New Zealand Soil Bureau Scientific Report No. 16, Department of Scientific and Industrial Research.

Lee, J. (1977) 'Land valuation should be based on productivity', *Farm and Food Research* **8**, 28–30.

Lex, L. A. and **Lex, L.** (1975) 'Land use control: the Black Hawk County experience', *Soil Conservation* **40**, 16–18.

Lindsay, J. D., Scheelar, M. D., and **Twardy, A. G.** (1973) 'Soil survey for urban development', *Geoderma* **10**, 35–45.

Loveday, J. (ed.) (1974) *Methods for analysis of irrigated soils*. Technical Communication No. 54, Commonweah Bureau of Soils.

Loveday, J., Beatty, H. J. and **Norris, J. M.** (1972) 'Comparison of current chemical methods for evaluating irrigation soils', Division of Soils Technical Paper No. 14, Commonwealth Scientific and Industrial Research Organisation, Australia.

Lynch, L. G. (1977) 'Input methods and facilities available for land survey data', in Moore, A. W. and Bie, S. W. (eds), *Uses of soil information systems*, Centre for Agricultural Publishing and Documentation, Wageningen, the Netherlands, pp. 11–18.

Lynch, L. G. and **Emery, K. A.** (1977) 'A regional information system for the Bathurst–Orange growth area', *Journal of the Soil Conservation Service of New South Wales* **33**, 43–46.

McCormack, D. E. (1974) 'Soil potentials: a positive approach to urban planning, *Journal of Soil and Water Conservation* **29**, 258–62.

McCormack, D. E. and **Bartelli, L. J.** (1977) 'Soils and land use – urban and suburban development', *Transactions of the American Society of Agricultural Engineers* **20**, 266–75.

McCormack, D. E., Moore, A. W. and **Dumanski, J.** (1978) 'A review of soil information systems in Canada, the United States, and Australia', *Symposia Papers, 11th International Congress of Soil Science*, Vol. 3, 143–56.

McGown, A. and **Iley, P.** (1973) 'A comparison of data from agricultural soil surveys with engineering investigations for roadworks in Ayrshire', *Journal of Soil Science* **24**, 145–56.

Mackney, D. (1974) 'Land use capability classification in the United Kingdom', in *Land capability classification*, Ministry of Agriculture, Fisheries and Food, Technical Bulletin No. 30, HMSO, pp. 4–11.

McRae, S. G. and **Burnham, C. P.** (1976) 'Soil classification', *Classification Society Bulletin* **3**, 56–64.

Mabbutt, J. A. (1968) 'Review of concepts of land classification', in Stewart, G. A. ed., *Land evaluation*, Macmillan of Australia, South Melbourne, pp. 11–28.

Maker, H. J., Downs, J. M. and **Anderson, J. U.** (1972) *Soil associations and land classification for irrigation, Sierra County*, Agricultural Experimental Station Research Report No. 233, New Mexico State University.

Makin, M. J. *et al.* (1976) *Prospects for irrigation development around Lake Zwai, Ethiopia*, Land Resource Study No. 26, Land Resources Development Centre, Ministry of Overseas Development, Surbiton, England.

Maletic, J. T. and **Hutchings, T. B.** (1967) 'Selection and classification of irrigable land' in Hagan, R. M. *et al.* (eds) *Irrigation of agricultural lands*, American Society of Agronomy, Madison, Wisconsin, pp. 125–73.

Mansfield, J. E. *et al.* (1975–76) *Land resources of the Northern and Luapula Provinces, Zambia – a reconnaissance assessment*, 6 vols, Land Resource Study No. 19, Land Resources Development Centre, Ministry of Overseas Development, Surbiton, England.

Manson, D. A. and **Greaves, B.** (1977) *Urban capability study: Banora Point–Tweed Heads*, Soil Conservation Service of New South Wales, Australia.

Mashimo, Y. (1974) 'Estimation of forest stand growth by quantification of soil conditions and environment factors', *Transactions 10th International Congress of Soil Science*, **6**, 50–5.

Matheson, G. D. and **Keir, W. G.** (1978) *Site investigation in Scotland*, Transport and Road Research Laboratory Report No. 828.

Mausel, P. W., Runge, E. C. A. and **Carmer, S. G.** (1975) 'Frequency distribution of tract productivity indexes and examples of their utilization in rural land assessment', *Proceedings Soil Science Society of America* **39**, 503–7.

Ministry of Agriculture, Fisheries and Food (1974) *Land capability classification*, Technical Bulletin No. 30, HMSO, London.

Mitchell, A. J. B. (1976) *The irrigation potential of soils along the main rivers of eastern Botswana: a reconnaissance assessment*, Land Resource Study No. 7, Land Resources Development Centre, Ministry of Overseas Development, Surbiton, England.

Mitchell, C. W. (1973) *Terrain evaluation*, Longman, London.

Montgomery, P. H. and **Edminster, F. C.** (1966) 'Use of soil surveys in planning for recreation', in Bartelli, L. J. *et al.* (eds), *Soil surveys and land use planning*, Soil Science Society of America and American Society of Agronomy, Madison, Wisconsin, pp. 104–112.

Moore, A. W. and **Bie, S. W.** (eds) (1977) *Uses of soil information systems*, Centre for Agricultural Publishing and Documentation, Wageningen, the Netherlands.

Morgan, J. P. (1974) 'A.D.A.S. (Lands) physical agricultural land classification', in *Land capability classification*, Ministry of Agriculture, Fisheries and Food, Technical Bulletin No. 30, HMSO, pp. 80–9.

Moss, R. P. (1968a) 'The ecological background to land use studies in tropical Africa with special reference to the west', in Thomas, M. F. and Whittington, G. W. (eds), *Environment and land use in Africa*, Methuen, London, pp. 193–238.

Moss, R. P. (1968b) 'An ecological approach to the study of soils and land use in the forest zone of Nigeria', in Thomas, M. F. and Whittington, G. W. (eds), *Environment and land use in Africa*, Methuen, London, pp. 385–407.

Moss, R. P. (1968c) 'Land use, vegetation and soil factors in south west Nigeria: a new approach', *Pacific Viewpoint* **9**, 107–27.

Moss, R. P. (1978) *Concept and theory in land evaluation for rural land use planning*, Occasional Publication No. 6, Department of Geography, University of Birmingham.

Murtha, G. G. and **Reid, R.** (1976) *Soils of the Townsville area in relation to urban development*, Division of Soils Divisional Report No. 11, Commonwealth Scientific and Industrial Research Organisation, Australia.

Nelson, L. A. *et al.* (1963) *Detailed land classification – island of Oahu*, University of Hawaii Land Study Bureau, Bulletin No. 3.

Nichols, J. D. and **Bartelli, L. J.** (1974) 'Computer-generated interpretive soil maps', *Journal of Soil and Water Conservation* **29**, 232–5.

Nortcliff, S. (1978) 'Soil variability and reconnaissance soil mapping: a statistical study in Norfolk', *Journal of Soil Science* **29**, 403–18.

Northcote, K. H. (1974) *A factual key for the recognition of Australian soils*, Rellim Technical Publications, Glenside, South Australia.

Nowland, J. L. (1978) 'Canada's agricultural land resource', paper presented at the 92nd Annual Conference Engineering Institute of Canada, St John's, Newfoundland, 25 May 1978. Land Resource Research Institute Contribution No. 2.

Olson, G. W. (1974) 'Land classifications', *Search, Agriculture* **4**, 1–34.

Ormiston, J. H. (1973) *Moray Firth: an agricultural study*, Special Report No. 9, Highlands and Islands Development Board, Inverness.

Papadakis, J. (ed.) (1952) *Agricultural geography of the world*, Buenos Aires.

Paterson, D. B. and **Webster, F.** (1977) 'Soil mapping for forest purposes in the North York Moors', *Proceedings North of England Soils Discussion Group* **9**, 1–19.

Patterson, G. T. and **Mackintosh, E. E.** (1976) 'Relationship between soil capability class and economic returns from grain corn production in southwestern Ontario', *Canadian Journal of Soil Science* **56**, 167–74.

Pawley, W. H. (1971) 'In the year 2070', *Ceres* **4**, 22–7.

Peters, T. W. (1977) 'Relationships of yield data to agroclimates, soil capability classification and soils of Alberta', *Canadian Journal of Soil Science* **57**, 341–7.

Pettry, D. E. and **Coleman, C. S.** (1973) 'Two decades of urban soil interpretations in Fairfax County, Virginia', *Geoderma* **10**, 27–34.

Peyer, K. *et al.* (1976) 'Bewässerungsplanung im Val, Müstair (GR) aufgrund von bodenkarten', *Schweizerische landwirtschaftliche Forschung* **15**, 361–9.

Presant, E. W. and **Wicklund, R. E.** (1971) *The soils of Waterloo County*, Report No. 44, Ontario Soil Survey, Ontario Department of Agriculture and Food, Toronto.

Pyatt, D. G., Harrison, D. and **Ford, A. S.** (1969) *Guide to site types in forests of north and mid-Wales*, Forestry Commission Forestry Record No. 69.

Raeside, J. D. and **Rennie, W. F.** (1974) *Soils of Christchurch region, New Zealand: the soil factor in regional planning*, New Zealand Soil Survey Report No. 16, Department of Scientific and Industrial Research, New Zealand.

Ragg, J. M. (1977) 'The recording and organization of soil field data for computer areal mapping', *Geoderma* **19**, 81–9.

Revelle, R. (1976) 'The resources available for agriculture', *Scientific American* **235**, 164–78.

Riquier, J. (1972) *A mathematical model for calculation of agricultural productivity in terms of parameters of soil and climate*, FAO, Rome.

Riquier, J. (1975) 'Present and future role of FAO in soil information systems', in Bie, S. W. (ed.) *Soil information systems*, Centre for Agricultural Publishing and Documentation, Wageningen, the Netherlands, pp. 79–83.

Riquier, J. and **Chidley, T. R. E.** (1978) 'The FAO international soil data bank', in Sadovski, A. N. and Bie, S. W. (eds) *Developments in soil information systems*, Centre for Agricultural Publishing and Documentation, Wageningen, the Netherlands, pp. 50–53.

Rudeforth, C. C. (1975) 'Storing and processing data for soil and land use capability surveys', *Journal of Soil Science* **26**, 155–68.

Rudeforth, C. C. and **Bradley, R. I.** (1972) *Soils, land classification and land use of west and central Pembrokeshire*, Special Survey No. 6, Soil Survey of England and Wales, Harpenden.

Russell, E. J. (1957) *The world of the soil*, Collins, London.

Russell, E. W. (1973) *Soil conditions and plant growth*, 10th edn, Longman, London.

Sadovski, A. N. and **Bie, S. W.** (eds) (1978) *Developments in soil information systems*, Centre for Agricultural Publishing and Documentation, Wageningen, the Netherlands.

Schelling, J. and **Bie, S. W.** (1978) 'Soil information systems – considerations for the future', *Symposia Papers, 11th International Congress of Soil Science*, Vol. 3, 208–13.

Simmons, I. G. (1974) *The ecology of natural resources*, Edward Arnold, London.

Simonson, R. W. (ed.) (1974) *Non-agricultural applications of soil surveys*, Elsevier, Amsterdam.

Smith, P. and **Sutherland, N. S.** (1974) 'Use of a land capability classification in a survey and development plan for the island of Mull', in *Land capability classification*, Ministry of Agriculture, Fisheries and Food, Technical Bulletin No. 30, HMSO, pp. 90–5.

Smith, R. T. and **Atkinson, K.** (1975) *Techniques in pedology*, Elek Science, London.

Smits, H. (n.d.) *Land reclamation in the former Zuider Zee in the Netherlands*, Rijksdienst voor de Ijsselmeerpolders, Lelystad, the Netherlands.

Soil Conservation Service, USDA (1973) *Pedon coding system for the National Cooperative Soil Survey,* Washington DC.

Soil resource inventories (1977) Agronomy Mimeo No. 77–23, Cornell University, Ithaca, New York.

Soil Survey Staff (1960) *Soil survey manual*, University States Department of Agriculture, Agriculture Handbook No. 18, Washington DC.

Soil Survey Staff (1975) *Soil taxonomy, a basic system*, United States Department of Agriculture, Agriculture Handbook No. 436, Washington DC.

Speight, J. G. (1968) 'Parametric description of land form', in Stewart, G. A. (ed.) *Land evaluation*, Macmillan of Australia, South Melbourne, pp. 239–50.

Stace, H. *et al.* (1968) *A handbook of Australian soils*, Rellim Technical Publications, Glenside, South Australia.

Stamp, L. D. (1962) *The land of Britain – its use and misuse*, 3rd edn, Longman, London.

Steur, G. G. L. (1961) 'Methods of soil surveying in use at the Netherlands Soil Survey Institute', *Boor en Spade* 11, 59–77.

Stewart, G. A. (ed.) (1968) *Land evaluation*, Macmillan of Australia, South Melbourne.

Storie, R. E. (1950) 'Rating soils for agricultural forest and grazing use', *Transactions 4th International Congress of Soil science* 1, 336–9.

Storie, R. E. (1954) 'Land classification as used in California for the appraisal of land for taxation purposes', *Transactions 5th International Congress of Soil Science* 3, 407–12.

Sys, C. and **Verheye, W.** (1974) 'Land evaluation for irrigation of arid regions by the use of the parameter method', *Transactions 10th International Congress of Soil Science* V, 149–55.

Thie, J. and **Ironside, G.** (eds) (1976) *Ecological (biophysical) land classification in Canada*, Ecological Land Classification Series No. 1, Lands Directorate.

Thomas, M. F. (1976) 'Purpose, scale and method in land resource surveys', *Geographia Polonica* **34**, 207–23.

Thomas, R. G. and **Thompson, J. G.** (1959) 'The classification and assessment of soils for irrigation in Southern Rhodesia', *Proceedings 3rd Inter-African Soils Conference*, pp. 345–50.

Toleman, R. D. L. (1974) 'Land classification in the Forestry Commission', in *Land capability classification*, Ministry of Agriculture, Fisheries and Food, Technical Bulletin No. 30, HMSO, pp. 97–108.

Trudgill, S. T. and **Briggs, D. J.** (1977) 'Soil and land potential', *Progress in Physical Geography* 1, 319–32.

Van Dam, J. G. C. (1973) *(Soil suitability research, in particular for asparagus, apples and hothouse tomatoes)* Bodemkundige Studies Nr 6, Mededelingen van de Stichting voor Bodemkartering, Wageningen, The Netherlands.

Van Dam, J. G. C. and **Zegers, H. J. M.** (1977) *Soil survey for grass sportsfields in the Netherlands*, Netherlands Soil Survey Institute, Wageningen, the Netherlands.

Van den Ban, J. P. A. (1964) 'Rural development in the river basin district', *Planning and Development in the Netherlands* **2**, 56–73.

Van Lier, H. N. (1972) 'Research on some technical aspects of outdoor recreation, as part of multipurpose rural reconstructions in the Netherlands', *Netherlands Journal of Agricultural Science* **20**, 154–79.

Van Liere, W. J. (1948) ('Soil conditions in the Westland'), *Verslagen van Landbouwkundige Onderzoekingen*, No. 54.6.

Van Onzenoort, A. A. H. C. (1973) 'Outdoor recreation planning in the Netherlands', *Planning and Development in the Netherlands* **7**, 50–63.

Vink, A. P. A. (1949) *(Contribution to the knowledge of loess and coversands, in particular of the southeastern Veluwe)*, Stichting voor Bodemkartering, Wageningen, the Netherlands.

Vink, A. P. A. (1963a) *Planning of soil surveys in land development*, Publication No. 10, International Institute for Land Reclamation and Improvement, Wageningen, the Netherlands.

Vink, A. P. A. (1963b) *(Some investigations on the soil suitability classification for arable and grassland farming)*, Bodemkundige Studies Nr 6, Mededelingen van de Stichting voor Bodemkartering, Wageningen, the Netherlands.

Vink, A. P. A. (1975) *Land use in advancing agriculture*, Springer-Verlag, Berlin.

Vink, A. P. A. and **van Zuilen, E. J.** (1974) 'The suitability of the soils of the Netherlands for arable land and grassland', Soil Survey Papers No. 8, Netherlands Soil Survey Institute, Wageningen, the Netherlands.

Watt, R. F. and **Newhouse, M. E.** (1973) 'Some soil phases in the Missouri Ozarks have similar site indexes for oaks', United States Department of Agriculture Forest Service Research Paper NC-86.

Webster, R. (1977) 'Soil survey: its quality and effectiveness', in *Soil resource inventories*, Agronomy Mimeo No. 77-23, Cornell University, Ithaca, New York, pp. 59–70.

Webster, R. and **Beckett, P. H. T.** (1970) 'Terrain classification and evaluation using air photography: a review of recent work at Oxford', *Photogrammetria* **26**, 51–75.

Weiers, C. J. (1975) 'Soil classification and land valuation', *Town and County Planning* **43**, 390–3.

Weiers, C. J. and **Reid, I. G.** (1974) *Soil classification, land valuation and taxation: the German experience*, Centre for European Agricultural Studies, Wye College, Ashford. Miscellaneous Studies No. 1.

Westerveld, G. J. W. and **van den Hurk, J. A.** (1973) 'Applications of soil and interpretive maps to non-agricultural land use in the Netherlands', *Geoderma* **10**, 47–65.

Whyte, R. C. (1976) *Land and land appraisal*, W. Junk, The Hague.

Wiken, E. G. and **Ironside, G. R.** (eds) (1977) *Ecological (biophysical) land classification in urban areas*, Ecological Land Classification Series No. 3, Lands Directorate.

Yager, T. U., Lee, C. A. and **Perfect, G. A.** (1967) *Report on the detailed soil survey and irrigability classification of the Chalimbana area, Zambia*, Soil Survey Report No. 1, Ministry of Agriculture, Republic of Zambia.

Young, A. (1973) 'Rural land evaluation', in Dawson, J. A. and Doornkamp, J. C. (eds) *Evaluating the human environment*, Edward Arnold, London, pp. 5–33.

Young, A. (1976) *Tropical soils and soil survey*, Cambridge University Press, Cambridge.

Young, A. (1978) 'Recent advances in the survey and evaluation of land resources', *Progress in Physical Geography* **2**, 462–79.

Young, A. and **Goldsmith, P. F.** (1977) 'Soil survey and land evaluation in developing countries: a case study in Malaŵi', *Geographical Journal* **143**, 407–31.

Zaporozec, A. and **Hole, F. D.** (1976) 'Resource suitability analysis in regional planning – with special reference to Wisconsin, USA', *Geoforum* **7**, 13–22.

Zayach, S. J. (1973) 'Soil surveys – their value and use to communities in Massachusetts', *Geoderma* **10**, 67–74.

Zonn, I. (1977) 'Irrigation of the world's arid lands', *World Crops and Livestock* **29**, 72–73.

INDEX